Acoustic Guitar:
Rhythm Essentials for the Advanced Beginner

Copyright © 2023 Lee Nichols
All rights reserved.
No portion of this book may be reproduced in any form without permission from the publisher.
Author Website www.guitar-chords.org.uk
Facebook: https://www.facebook.com/guitarchordsandmore/

Contents

Introduction 3
Rhythm and Timing 5
Timing, Feel and Counting 7
Strumming Patterns 12
Dynamics 16
Bass and Strum 19
Melodic Rhythm / Arpeggios 21
Slow / Fast Strum 23
Partial Chord Strumming 26
Muting and Muted Strums 29
6/8 and 12/8 36
Shuffle Rhythms 39
Changing Chords - Keeping the Flow 44
Backing Tracks and Chords 47
Example Song 1 48
Example Song 2 51
Example Song 3 54
Example Song 4 57
Example Song 5 60
Example Song 6 63
Example Song 7 66
Example Song 8 69
Example Song 9 71
Example Song 10 74
Where Next 77
Audio Downloads 78

Introduction

What's this book about and who is it for?

This book is in the style of a short course and focuses on improving your acoustic guitar rhythm playing. Although not limited to acoustic, you could equally apply the same techniques to electric guitar, but this book is written with the acoustic guitar in mind and the examples are based on the kind of rhythms that are typically suited to acoustic guitar rhythms.

Whether you play alone or jam with others, playing with a solid rhythm with the correct feel makes all the difference. Learning to play in time, with good rhythm technique and the right feel, is all you need to be able to stand out and confidently jam along with others.

I see many common problems with amateur guitarists that can be easily rectified with a little practice, bringing you to the "driving seat" of the jam or band instead of hiding awkwardly in the background.

Acoustic jam nights, open mics etc, are now very common. Not only are they fun, but they are also a great place to learn and improve. Most of these kinds of jams use standard songs that are easy enough to follow, more often than not, consisting of just three chords. These are usually chord progressions in open position like C, F, G or G, C, D and often in the style of Country, Folk, Campfire / sing-along etc.

These types of tunes lend themselves very well to using a capo for other keys, in fact, many of them sound better with the capo rather than using closed or moveable chord positions because it maintains the open chord sound, which is often we want. This is great because it allows us to concentrate our practice time on what's most important without spreading the learning curve too thin.

Is this suitable for Beginners?

Sort of. This is the first in a series of short books designed to take you from advanced beginner to a competent, and more advanced, rhythm player, able to play along with others, either driving the jam or adding something worthwhile and noticeable to it. The problem here is many people have different ideas of what a beginner is. I personally don't like the term because it's undefined. Let's just say if you have only just picked up the guitar and started learning, then you are a **complete beginner**. If you can play the common open chords such as A, Am, C, D, Dm, E, G and play some basic strum patterns without your fingers stumbling, then you are perhaps an **intermediate beginner**. If you can play all of the open chords, the common moveable bar chords, such as F and Bb, able to play a good variation of strumming patterns then you are maybe an **advanced beginner** or higher, perhaps into the intermediate levels.

This book falls somewhere between the last two levels. It's not for the complete beginner but somewhere between intermediate and advanced beginner. You should at the very least be able to play the basic open chords and the F chord, whether that's fully or partially barred. I will be giving some tips here and there, but generally, I won't be telling you how to hold the guitar or how to place your fretting hand fingers to play a common chord. As long as you can read a chord diagram and guitar Tablature then you shouldn't have any problems.

Rhythm and Timing

Let's quickly talk about the most obvious thing of all - strumming the guitar in time with good rhythm. This is absolutely the most important skill of all, but it often gets overlooked and a lot of guitarists struggle with it, sometimes without even realising. In my experience of watching and listening to others, I see this generally caused by a common problem - the strumming hand is not consistent in its repetition and has nothing guiding it, in other words, the rhythm hand loses its place.

For example, music is broken up into bars. In 4/4 music we have four beats to the bar, which we count "one - two - three - four". We may sometimes divide each beat into two, or four giving us eighth notes and sixteenth notes. We can count these as "one and two and three and four" for eighth notes and something like "one e and a two e and a ..." and so on (more on this later). When we count out loud like this, we have the actual words guiding us, they keep our place in the music. Every time we say "one" we know we're at the start of a new bar. Every time we say "two" or "four" we know we're on the so-called backbeat.

If we count in our head the whole time we are playing, then we have a guide. In reality we don't always do that, we might mentally side-track or we might be singing at the same time. No musician plays without some sort of guide like this. With experience it can just become a subconscious feel, but it always needs to be there.

Our rhythm / strumming hand still needs to be guided in some way and it's usually led by repetitive patterns. This pattern can be created in many ways, not necessarily just by the up and down strums. It can be dynamic variation, the strings we hit, where we play them, how we play them or any number of things.

Here's where I think one of the biggest problems lie - the up and down strums get messed up. Generally speaking, we play a down-strum on the down-beat and an up-strum on the up-beat. This isn't a rule but let's just say for simplicity, this means down-strum on the "one, two, three and four" and up-strum for all the "ands". If we aren't properly paying attention (I see this happen a lot), then the ups and downs sometimes trip up. This can happen for any number of reasons but it's usually some sort of hesitation which might result in a down-strum being played where it should be an up-strum (or vice-versa) and things can start to get messy.

Of course, there can be other reasons but overall, everything is too rigid. We need our strumming hand to work on autopilot and this is helped by repetitive patterns, articulations, dynamics etc. In short, the strumming hand needs more to work with than a rigid, or highly repetitive, up-down strum with no variation.

Now I might be labouring the point here, but it really is important that you fully grasp this. We can demonstrate these problems by simply saying them out loud.
Try saying "boom boom boom boom boom boom boom boom" repeatedly, in a consistent time and volume. In your head you will probably be thinking of them in groups of four. It may be

thirty seconds, maybe five minutes, but eventually you will probably lose your place. Not necessarily a massive problem, you might lose where the "one" is but you should still be saying it in a consistent time.

Now try the same again but saying "Boom chuka Boom chuck, Boom chuka Boom chuck". You might eventually lose your place but only because it will drive you insane. But for as long as you keep going, you will always know where you are within the phrase, you'll either be on the Boom (one and three), chuka (two-and) chuck (four).

When your strumming is inconsistent you may end up doing the spoken equivalent of something like this ... Boom bah boom bah boom bah boom bah boom bah bah boom bah. When you get to the double "bah bah" it's the equivalent of your up and down strum going out of phase. The problem is not necessarily the wrong strum direction, it's possible to continue playing in time and then correct it in the next bar or two. In reality, however, it causes hesitation because we instinctively strum down on the down-beat and everything starts to feel wrong, we then try to play catch up but the end result is we've lost or place and also our timing and feel.

In the next chapter we will look at various strumming patterns and techniques that help to avoid this problem.

Timing, Feel and Counting

Playing rhythm with the correct time and feel. This is fairly basic stuff, yet it's very important to properly get to grips with. Get this right and your rhythm playing will take on a whole new dimension. Not only will you sound better, but it will also help to improve your timing and not lose your place within a song.

There are many ways this can be done, but before we get to that, let's start with the difference between 3/4 and 4/4.

For a very rough and quick explanation - music is divided into bars, and bars are divided into beats. This we call the time signature.
4/4 music has four beats to the bar.
3/4 music has three beats to the bar.
There are other time signatures we'll look at later, but we'll just deal with these two for the moment.

There is also "feel" which can describe how the beats are divided, for example, a straight or triplet feel, but we'll also get to that later. For now, the following examples are all in straight feel.

The tempo is measured by BPM which means beats per minute. At 60BPM each beat will last for one second. At 120BPM there will be two beats per second. Therefore, if we have a piece of music in 4/4 at 60BPM, each bar will last four seconds. At 120BPM each bar will last for two seconds. In 3/4 the beats will last the same length but there will only be three per bar, therefore at 60BPM each bar will last three seconds and at 120BPM a bar will last 1.5 seconds.

When we play a piece of music, we need to be able to hear how the bars and beats are divided. If not then we have nothing guiding us. This can be dictated by the drums, the melody or any of the other instruments but it isn't always immediately obvious, depending on the song and how it's played. We need some kind of repetitive pattern that is giving us the time and the feel otherwise everything can become very messy.

For example, if we repeatedly strum a chord twice every second but have no variation breaking up the pattern then there is no way for us to know what the time or feel is. It could be either 3/4 or 4/4 at 120BPM playing 1/4 notes or it could be at 60BPM playing 1/8th notes. It could also be that it should have a shuffle or triplet feel but it isn't being outlined. Here we'll take a quick look at 1/4, 1/8th and 1/16th notes just in case you're not quite sure what it all means. Shuffle feel we'll look at a bit later in the book.

Audio examples are available at the web address shown at the end of this book. If you are reading the eBook version then, depending on your reader, you may be able to click on each example to open it up in your browser, if not just go to the downloads page.
Take a listen to the audio for an example of a strum pattern with no variation. It sounds messy

and gives us no indication of the time or feel.

Listen to **Example 1**

The following examples will all be using the standard C major chord for demonstration.

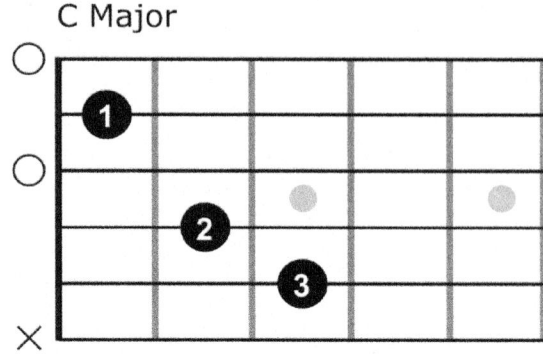

Counting 1/4 notes in 4/4 time

We should always be able to count the timing out loud, or in our heads. It's the best way to describe and understand various rhythms. In 4/4 at 60BPM, each beat lasts for one second and there's four beats in each bar so we count "one two three four" in time with each beat. This completes the bar, we then repeat one to four for each bar.

Here's how it looks in TAB for four bars - first bar with metronome only, then one bar with counting and metronome followed by counting, metronome and 1/4 note strums.

Example 2

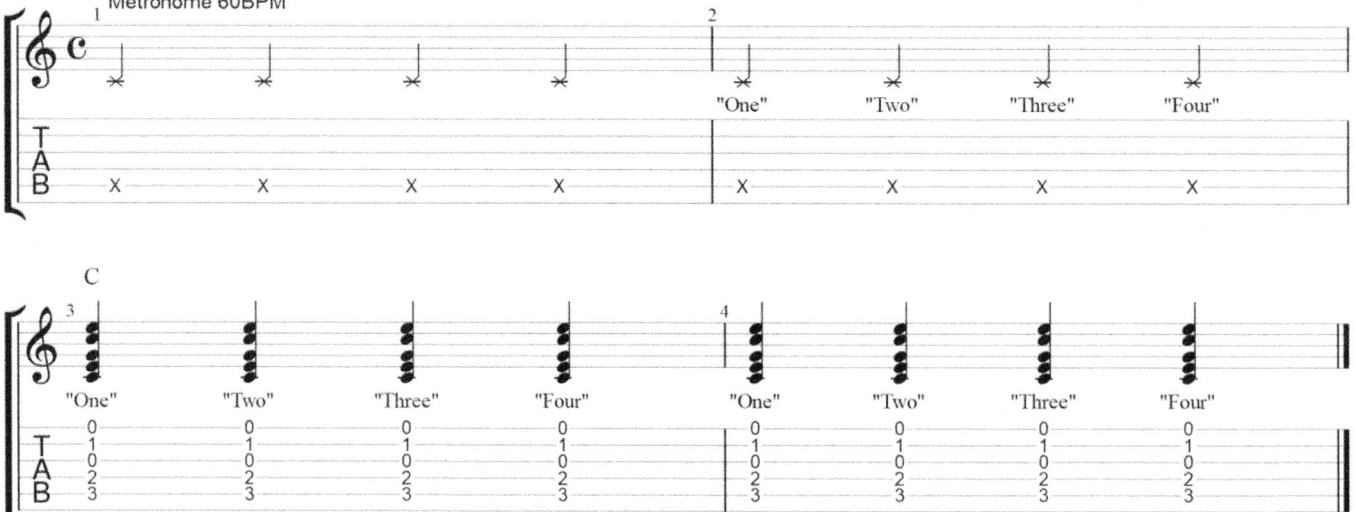

Counting 1/4 notes in 3/4 time

In 3/4 time there are only three 1/4 notes to the bar and we count them "one two three". This terminology can be a bit confusing, i.e., four "quarter" notes per bar makes sense but three "quarter" notes per bar sounds a bit strange, you could be forgiven for thinking they should be called thirds. In the UK the 1/4 note is usually called a crotchet, but because of things like the internet and YouTube, it's becoming more commonly known as a "quarter note". We don't want to complicate things here by getting too deep into theory so for the most part - just think of the term "quarter note" as meaning "beat".

Below is how things look and sound in 3/4 timing.

Example 3

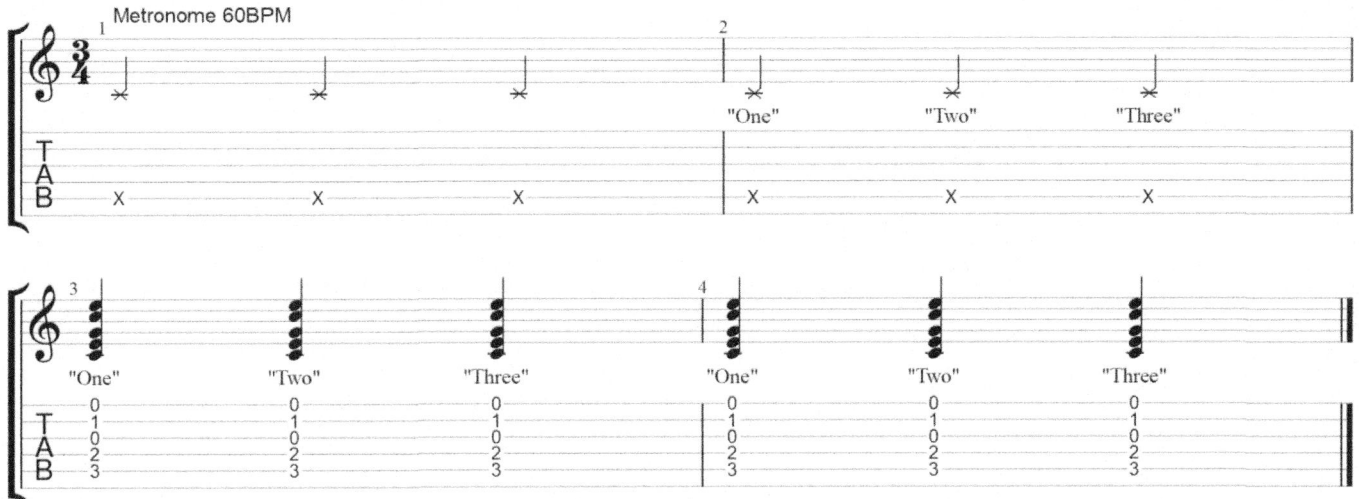

1/8th and 1/16th notes

We can divide each beat into two or four giving us eight notes per bar or sixteen notes per bar.
For 1/8th notes we count with the word "and" between each 1/4 note beat, i.e., "one and two and three and four".
For 1/16th notes we can use "e" and "a" before and after the "and", like this ...
"One e and a two e and a three e and a four e and a"
The following examples are shown in 4/4 time only but the same also applies to 3/4.

Example 4 - 8th notes

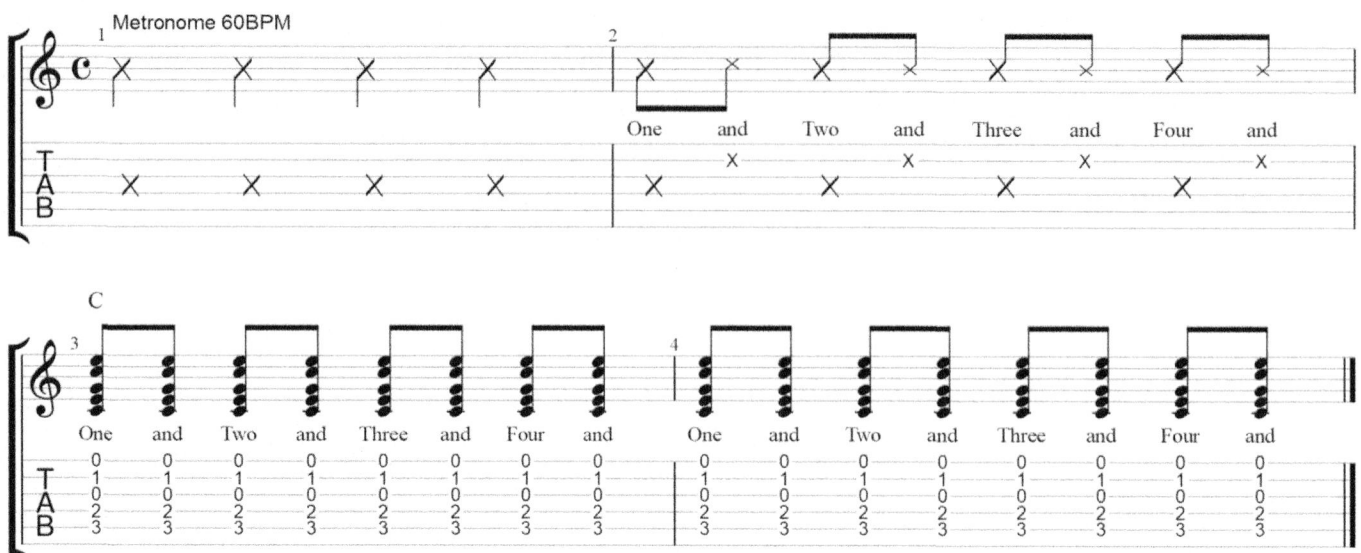

Example 5 - 16th notes

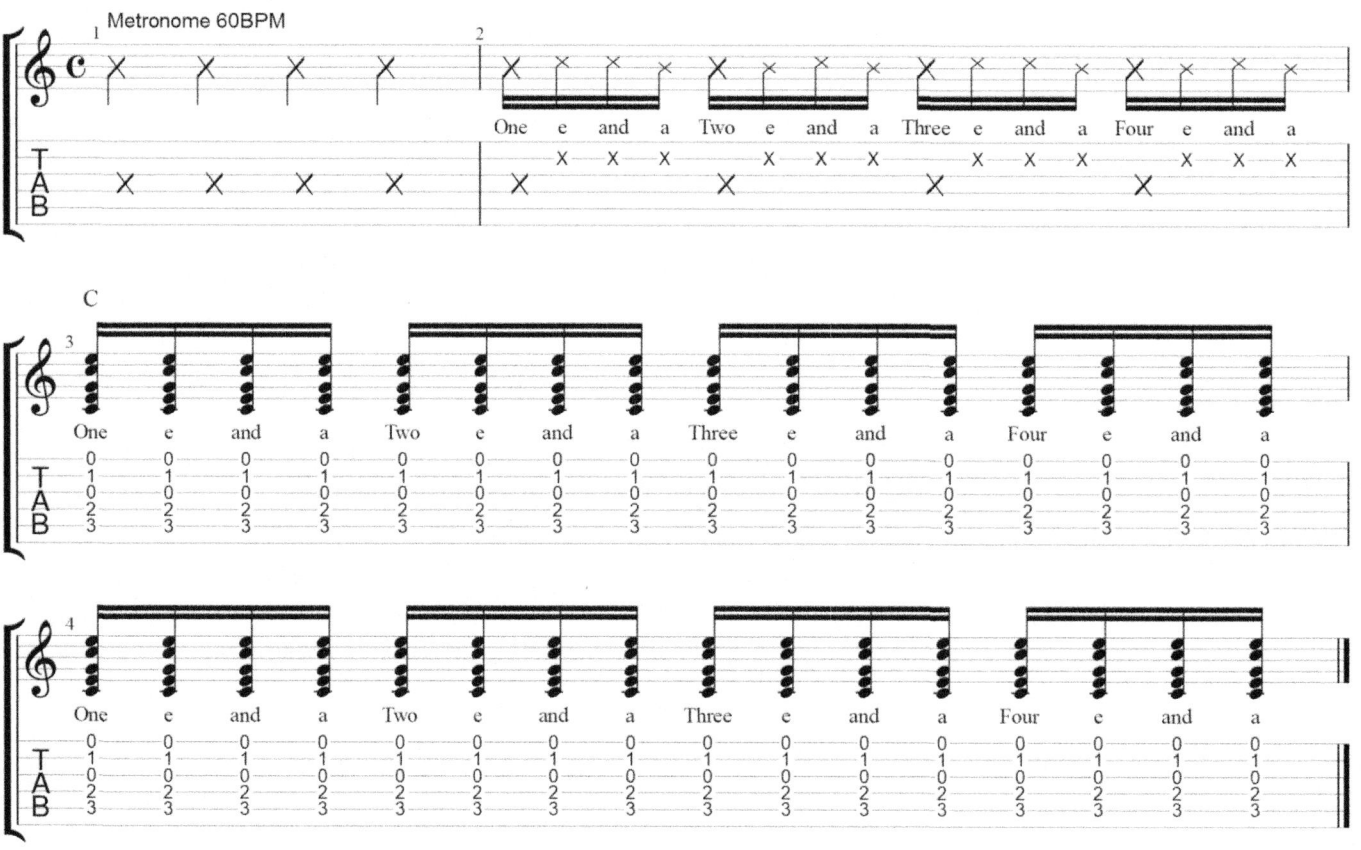

Counting like this helps us keep track and make sense of the rhythms. We don't however count like this when we're playing in a real-life situation. It's good for practice and it's a necessity for count-ins to start a song. Beyond this, however, we need to be able to hear it in the rhythm or melodic patterns from the other instruments, possibly even you being the one leading it on the guitar. A drummer for instance may play something as simple as kick-snare-kick-snare for 4/4. From this we'll always know the kick is one and three, the snare is two and four. They might play the kick harder on the first beat of each bar and softer on the third beat. More often than not, the high-hat will be playing along with the kick and snare which might be played closed on beats one to three but open on beat four - this way we hear the open high-hat and know that the following beat will be the "one" of the next bar.

That's all very simplified and most drum patterns will be more involved, but this will be the basis of things for most songs. If you listen to the drums, you should easily get a sense of whether we are in 3/4 or 4/4 and where each beat lies within the bar.

To some extent we still need to keep track of things in our heads but if for some reason we get lost, it should be easy enough for us to fall back into place by listening to what the other musicians are doing. As a guitarist, this means we should also be doing our bit to make our rhythm playing reflect the time and feel. Even if we are the only musician playing, creating this same sense of rhythm is still vitally important - pretty much all music needs a proper sense of rhythm. If we are playing along with others, then it really is a necessity otherwise it can be very off-putting for everybody else trying to play along with you.

None of this needs to be complicated or difficult to learn, we can play very simple rhythms, something like a single strum once on each 1/4 note beat. This is easy to play and stay in time, but more importantly won't cause any problems for other musicians that might be playing along with you. The only rhythm you want to avoid at all times is a continuous up / down strum in 1/8th notes all at constant volume with no variation - like the one in the audio Example 1. A rhythm like this will drive everyone crazy, not just the other musicians but also the listener too.

In the next chapter we'll look at some of the ways we can play rhythm patterns that reflect the time signature.

Strumming Patterns

Most tutorials for the beginner guitarist talk about the up / down strumming patterns. There's actually a lot more we can, and should, do to play better and more interesting rhythms, but first let's talk about the Down and Up strum.

The down strum and the up strum do sound slightly different which creates some variation in the sound of our rhythm. Generally speaking (but not a rule), the down / up refers to placement within the rhythm. We play a down-strum on the "one, two three and four" and an up-strum for the "ands" (often referred to as the "down beat" and the "up beat"). Therefore a 4/4 pattern that looks like this:
Down Down Down Up Down ... would have a rhythm pattern that we'd count like this:
One Two Three and Four One two three and four

This is best understood with examples. D and U are used for the Down and Up strums in the TAB.

Example 6

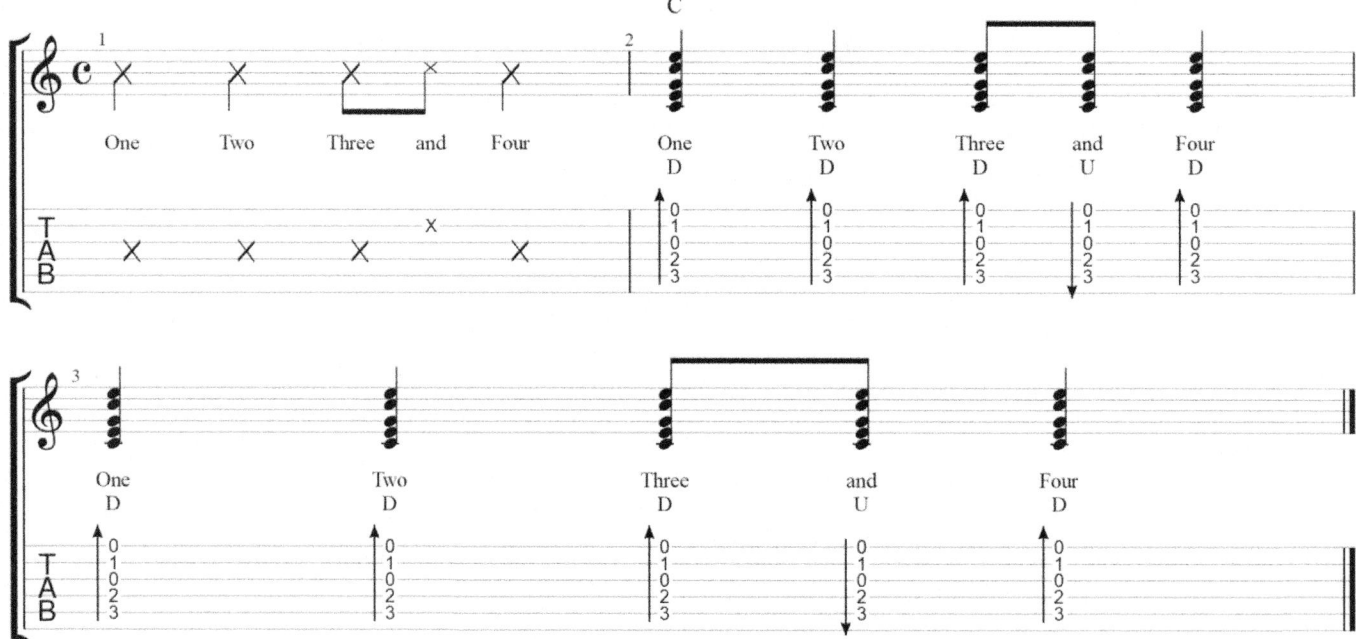

Some variations:

Example 7

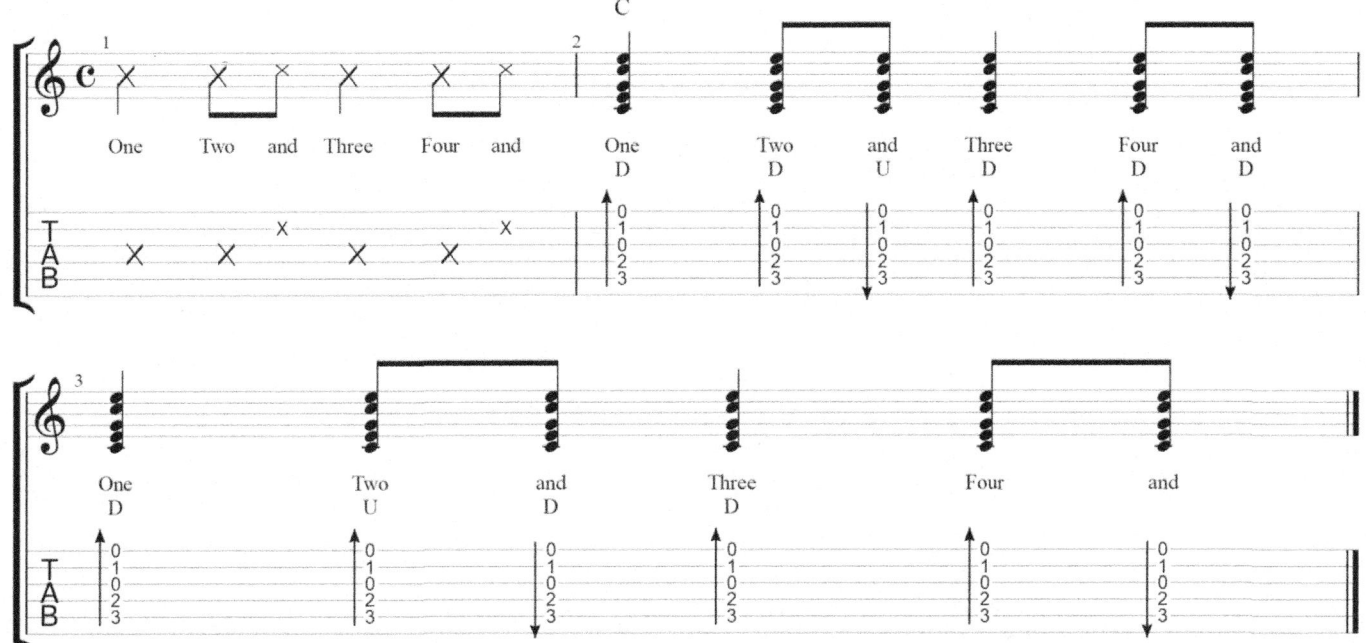

Example 8

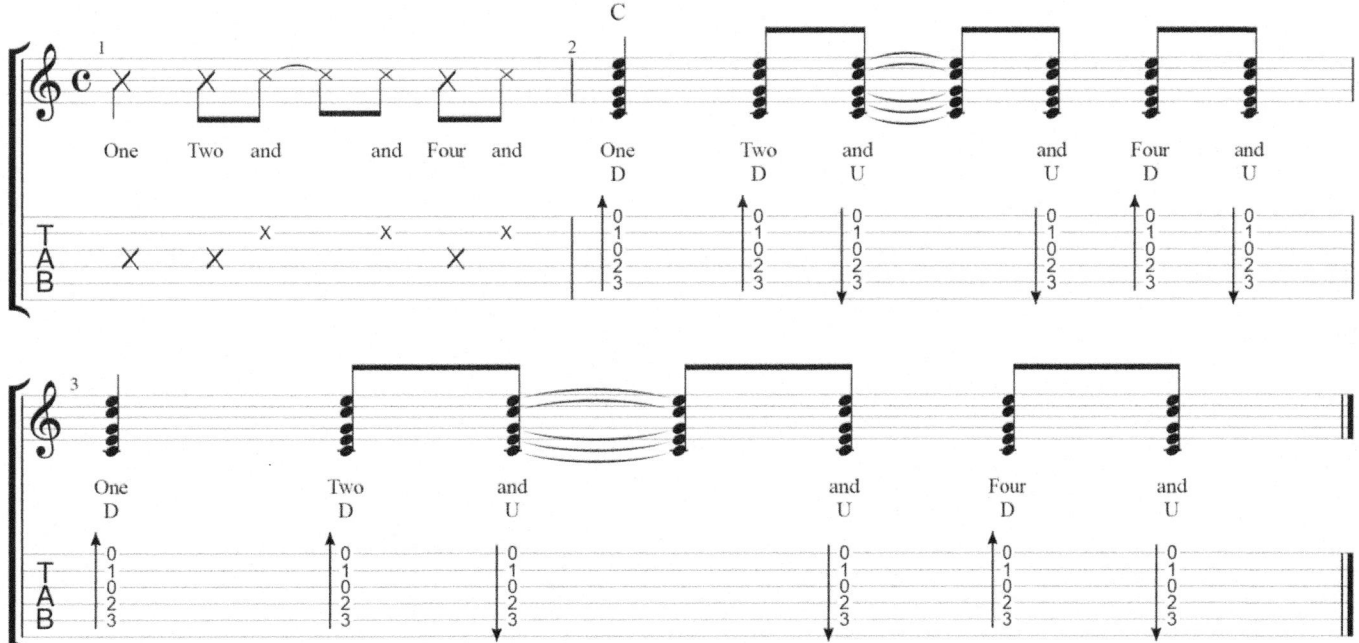

Example 9

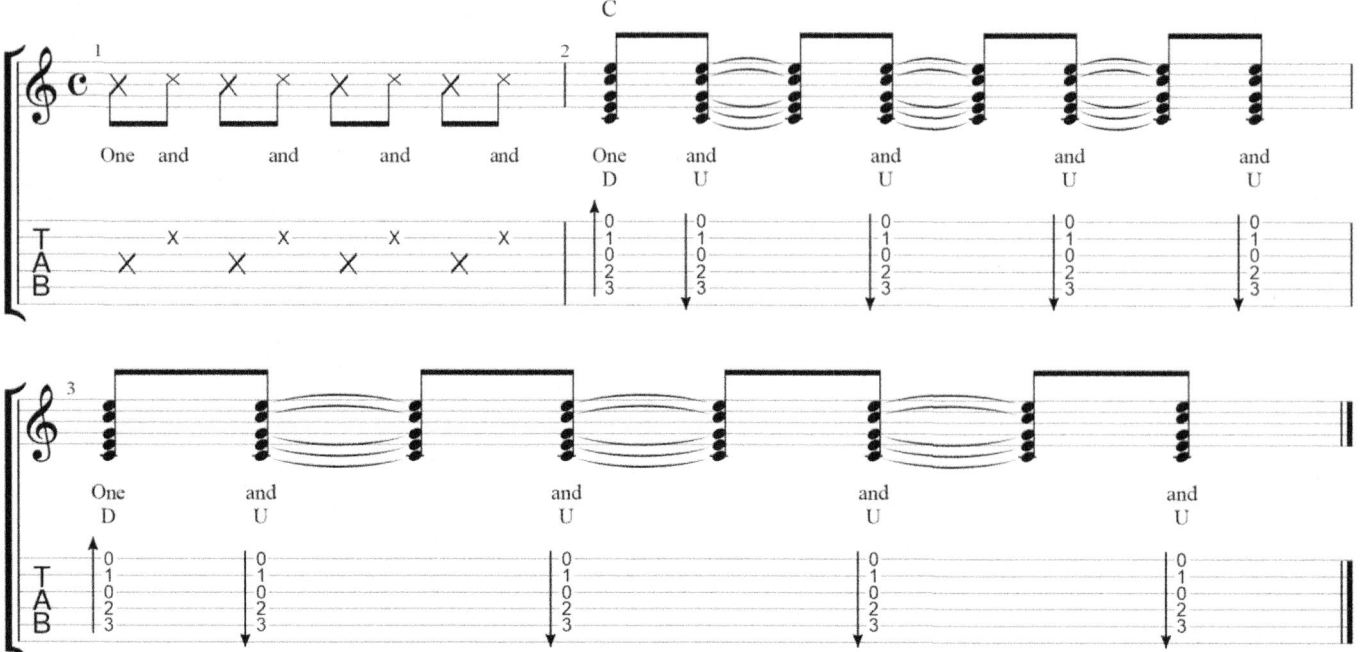

These Down up rhythms are often written something like DDUUDU and they assume all 1/8th notes. They're OK for learning the concept but don't rely on them too much as they don't help with more complex patterns.

For 3/4 we do the same thing but with just three beats so our pattern might be something like example 10 - Down Down Down Up - counted as One Two Three And One Two Three And (DDDU) or example 11 - Down Down UP Down UP(DDUDU).

Example 10

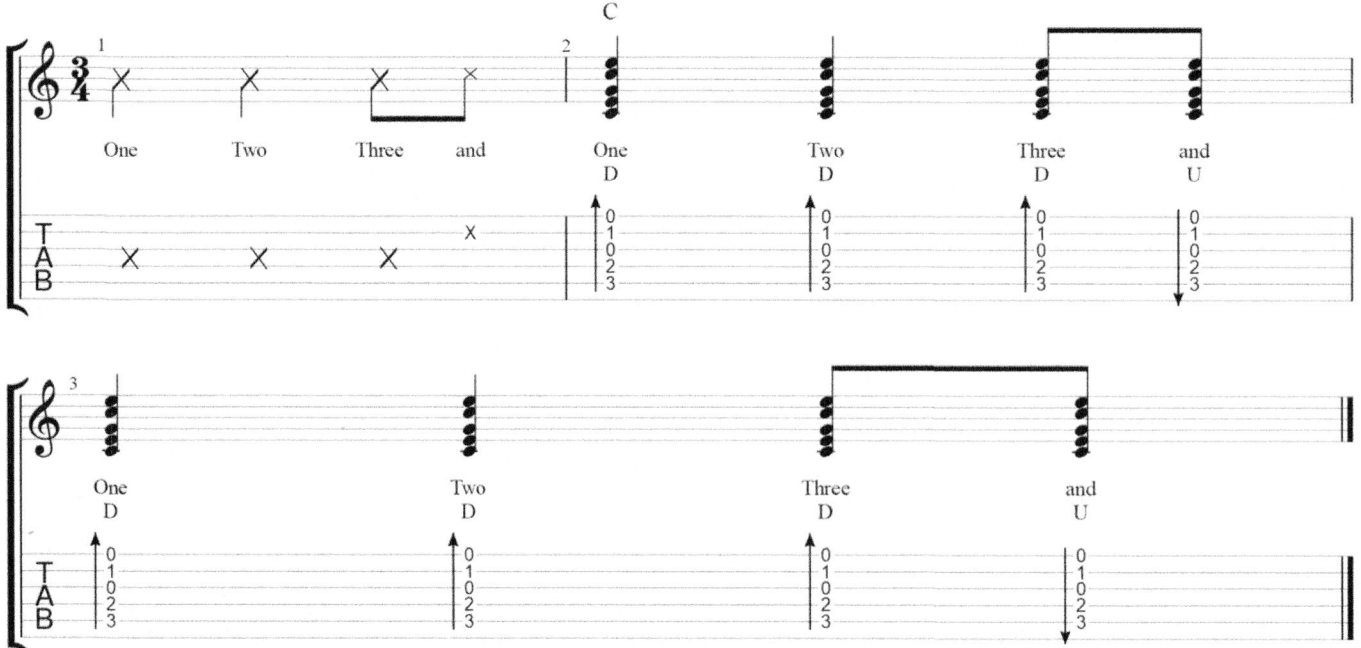

Example 11

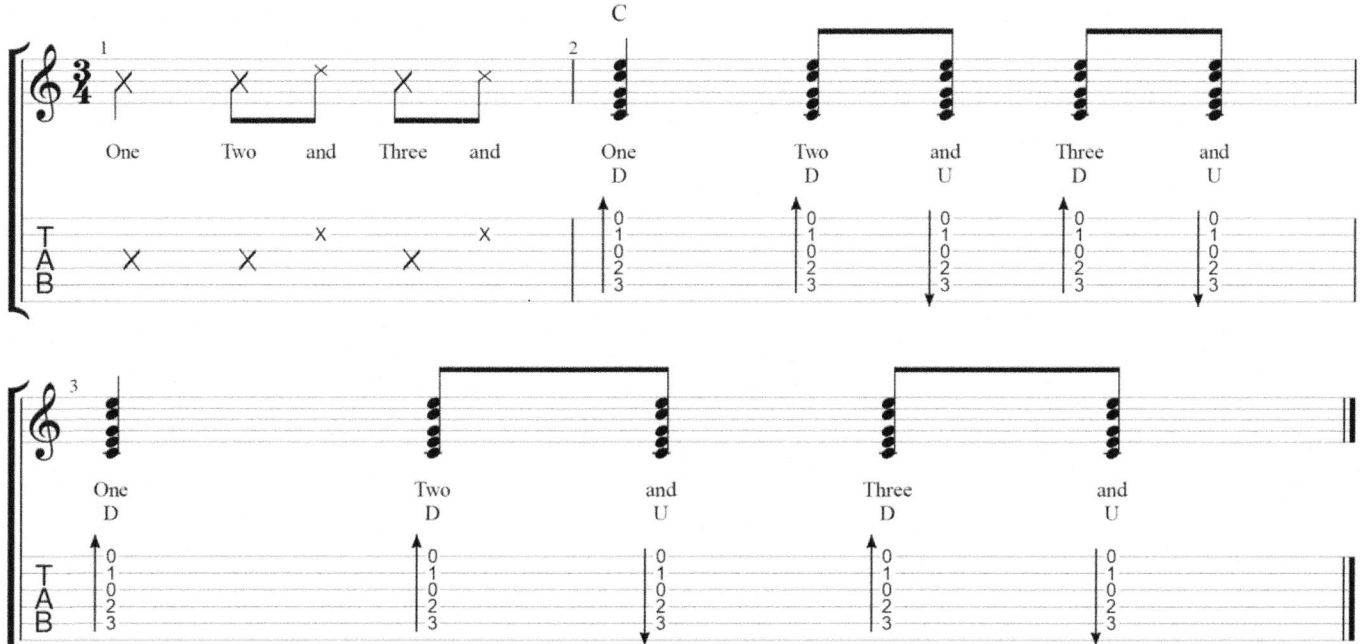

As we can see in the examples, we create repeating patterns which gives us a sense of the time signature. If we're not sure whether a song is 3/4 or 4/4 then this is how we know. We listen out for these repetitions, not necessarily from just the guitar, it can be any, or all, of the instruments creating the feel and timing.

These repetitions don't need to be purely based on time, they could also be dynamic or melodic variations. We can create repeatable patterns in many other ways - all of them can go towards helping create better and more interesting rhythms. The more you learn and practise, the more choices you will have to vary your playing.

We'll look at these in the following chapters.

Dynamics

In the previous chapter we looked at using a mixture of 1/4 and 1/8th notes to create varying rhythms and give us a sense of the timing and repetition, i.e., whether we're playing in 3/4 or 4/4.

There are many other ways we can create the same effect and add variation to our rhythm. We're going to look at some of these over the next few chapters - some are easy, some will take more practice. We'll start with dynamics.

Dynamics refers to volume. It's an easy but effective technique that should always be a part of your playing.

On the guitar, if we accent certain notes or strums by playing them harder, then we create rhythms with a mix of hard / soft. Although I use the terms hard and soft, that's not quite what we want, it's more like normal and then a bit softer or a bit louder. We're just looking to play with varying amounts of loudness to create repeatable patterns or variation in our rhythm. This doesn't really need much explaining so we'll just go ahead and look at examples. Be sure to listen to the audio examples, note we don't want to go mad, it's quite subtle, but audible differences we're aiming for.

In the TABs we use > below the notes to indicate an accent (play louder). We can also use a V like symbol to indicate a heavy accent. In other words, > = louder and V = Louder still.

Accented notes in notation

Example 12 - 3/4 just quarter notes - hard soft soft

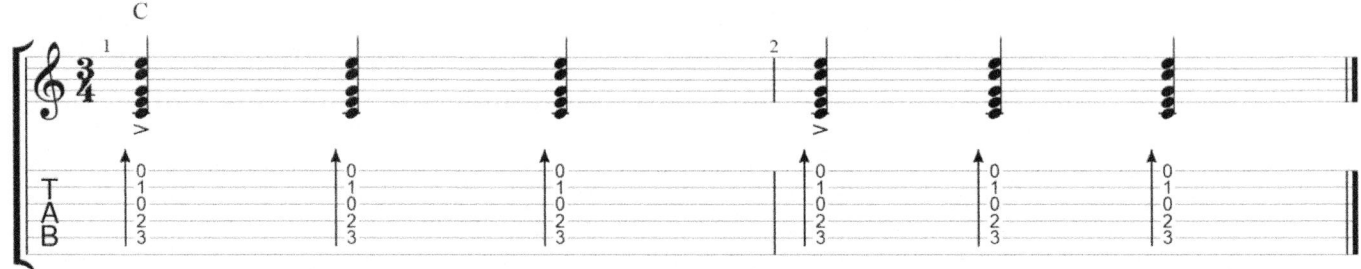

Example 13 - 4/4 just quarter notes Hard soft soft soft

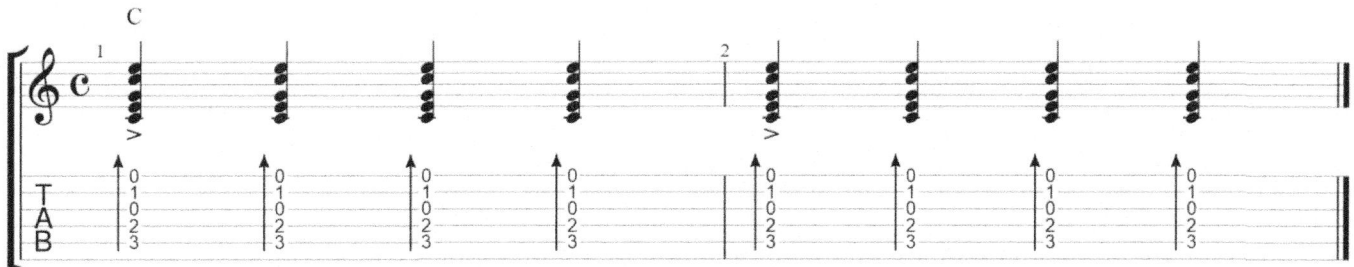

Example 14 - 4/4 just quarter notes Hard soft Hard soft - this one doesn't give us a sense of beat one but it's a common rhythm that works well when another instrument is providing the time.

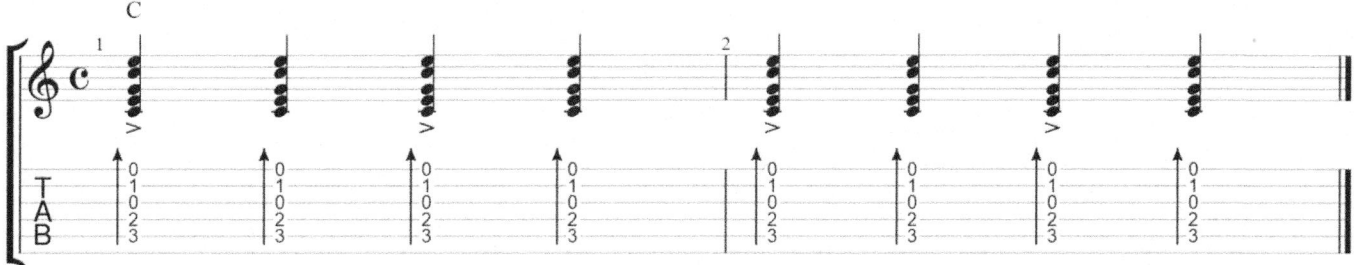

Example 15 - 4/4 just quarter notes Hard soft less-hard soft - this one is more subtle.

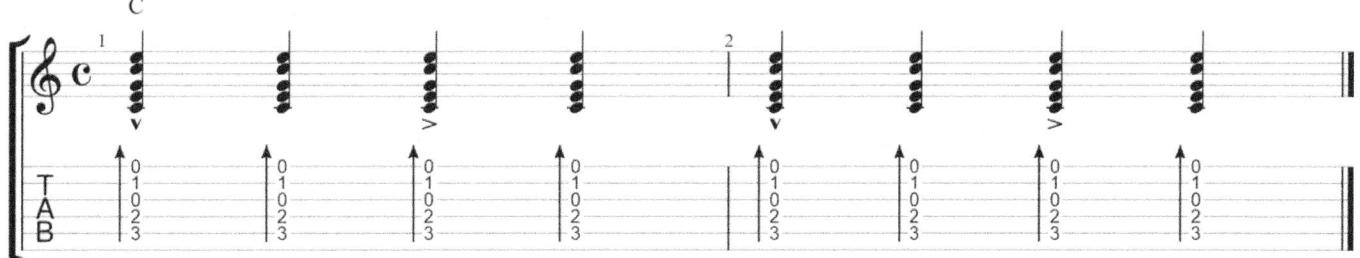

All of these can be mixed up with 1/8 notes, for example

Example 16

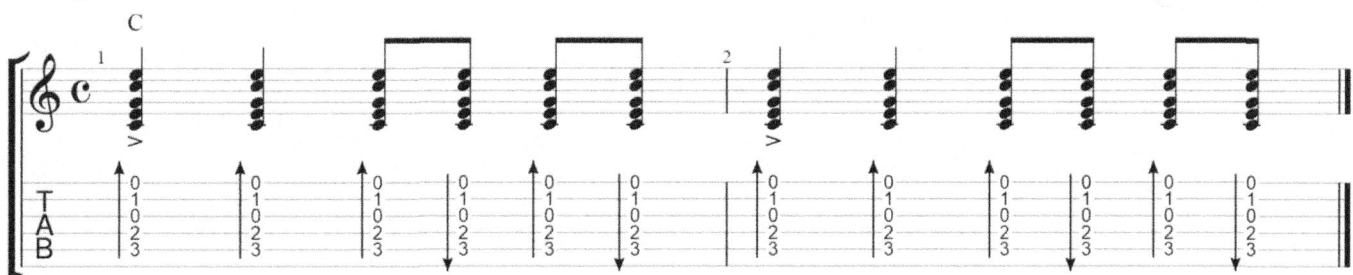

These are just things to become familiar with and practise. Eventually we'll be combining this with other ideas and techniques to make more interesting rhythms. Although it's quite common to play harder on each first beat of the bar, another common rhythm is to play harder on the two and four, this gives us a sense of backbeat where the snare would often be played.

Example 17 - Accents on the 2 and 4.

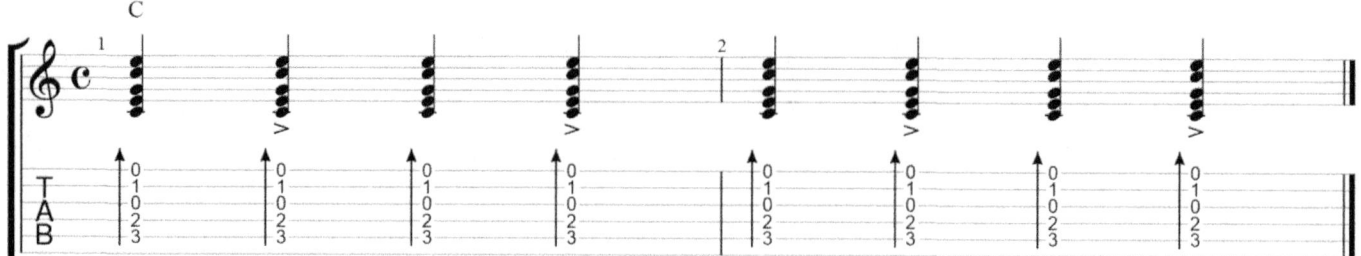

Bass and Strum

Another very common rhythm technique is to pick a single bass note followed by a strum, or alternate between two bass notes. This is very often used in old-time country styles but will work for other genres too. Here are some examples using the C chord.

Example 18 - 4/4 Bass(C) Strum strum strum

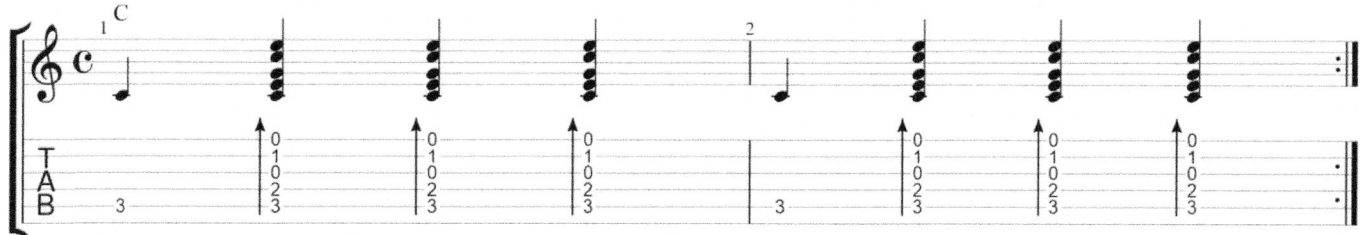

Example 19 - 3/4 Bass(C) Strum strum

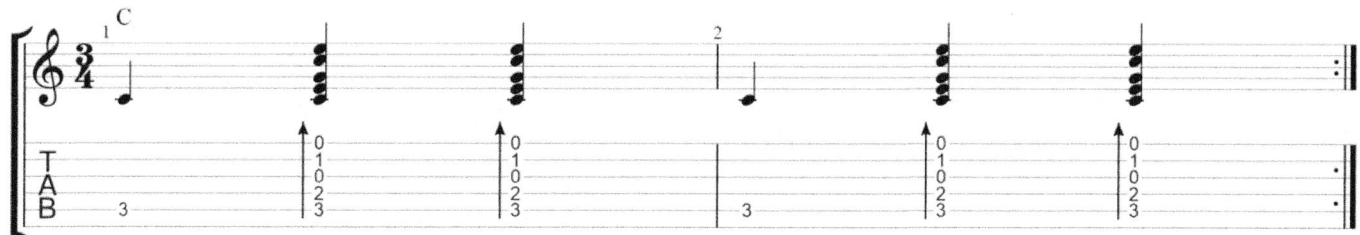

Example 20 - 4/4 Alternate C Strum G Strum. (C and G refers to the picked bass notes)

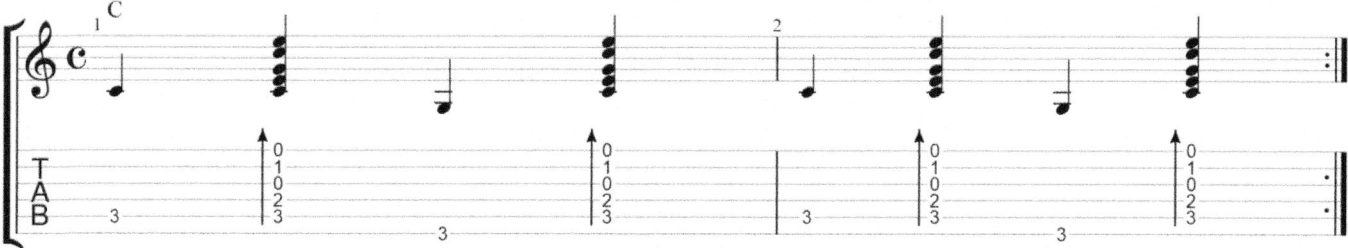

Example 21 - 3/4 Alternate C Strum Strum G strum strum

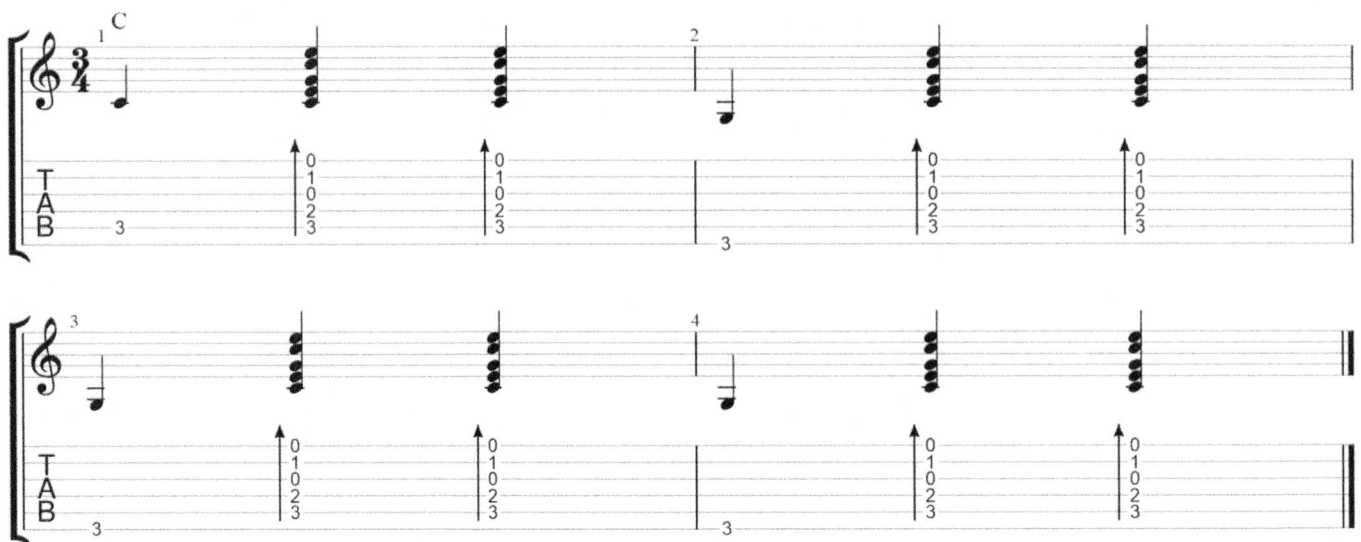

Example 22 - 4/4 Alternate C Strum G Strum with some 1/8 note up strokes

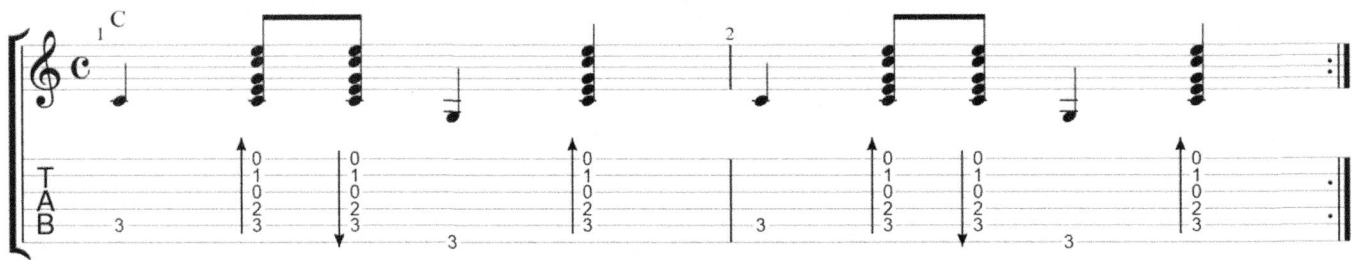

Example 23 - 3/4 variation of above

We can go a lot further with this technique by adding more bass fills and runs between chords, but this will be for another book in the series.

Melodic Rhythm / Arpeggios

An arpeggio is how we describe a chord played one note at a time instead of all notes strummed at once. Below are a few examples. We don't need to play the notes in any specific order, nor do we need to play all of the notes on each string. Just hold the chord down as normal but pick notes out individually.

Example 24 - 4/4 Example playing all of the notes in the C chord ascending then descending.

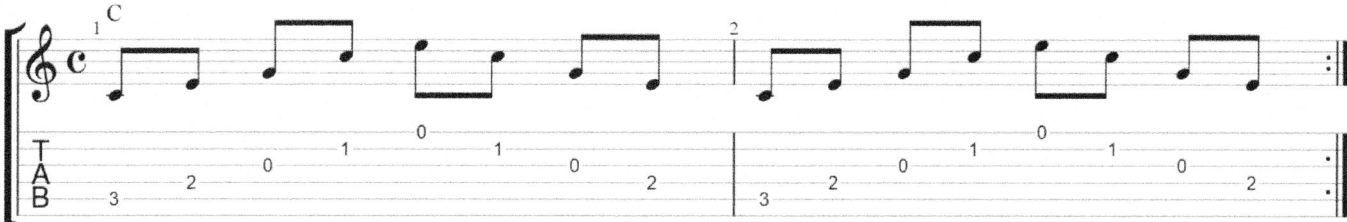

Example 25 - Pattern variation not using the high E string.

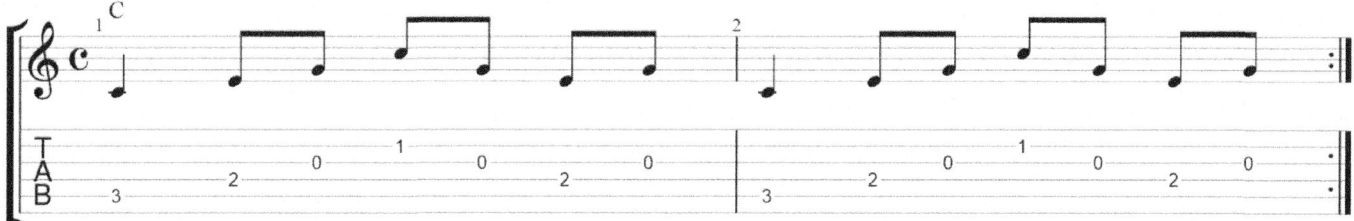

Example 26 - 3/4 Ascending / descending pattern

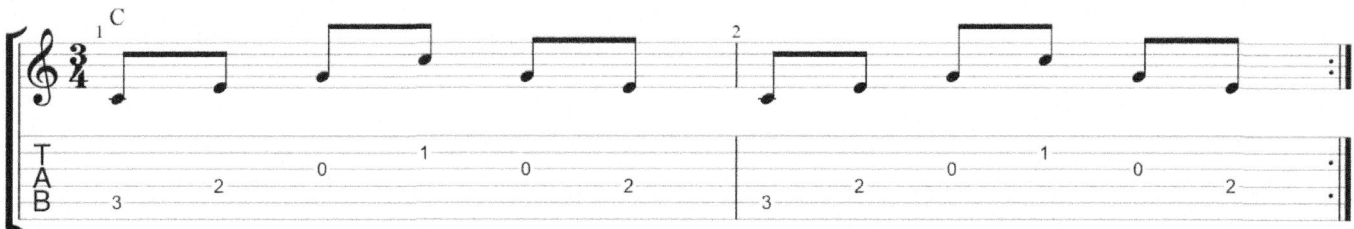

Example 27 - 3/4 pattern using only the bottom three strings of the chord

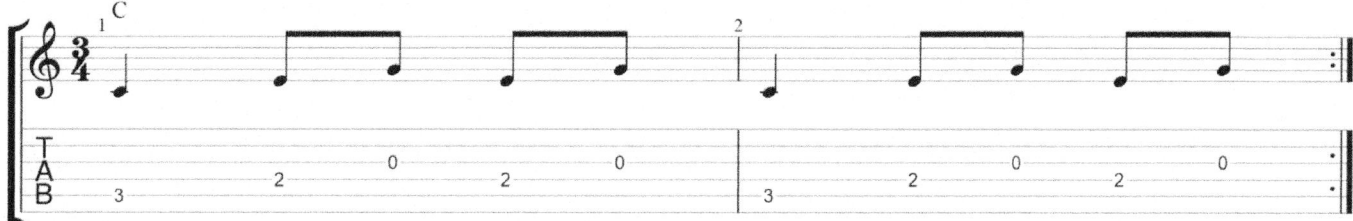

We can also mix arpeggio playing with chord strumming, here's a few examples:

Example 28 - 4/4 Strum / pick

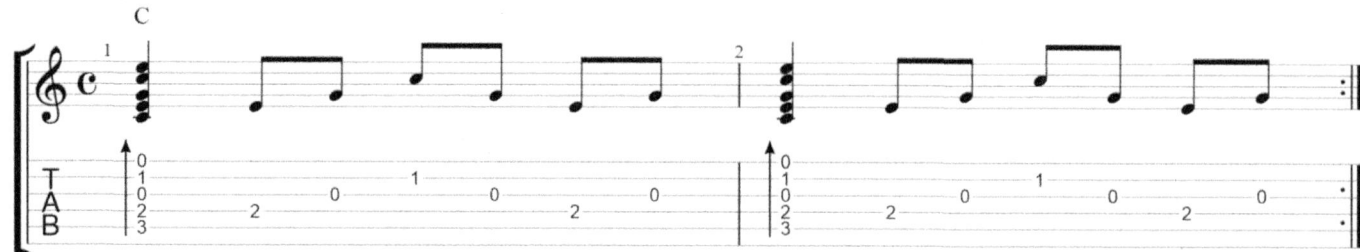

Example 29 - 4/4 Bass / Strum / pick

Example 30 - 3/4 Strum / pick

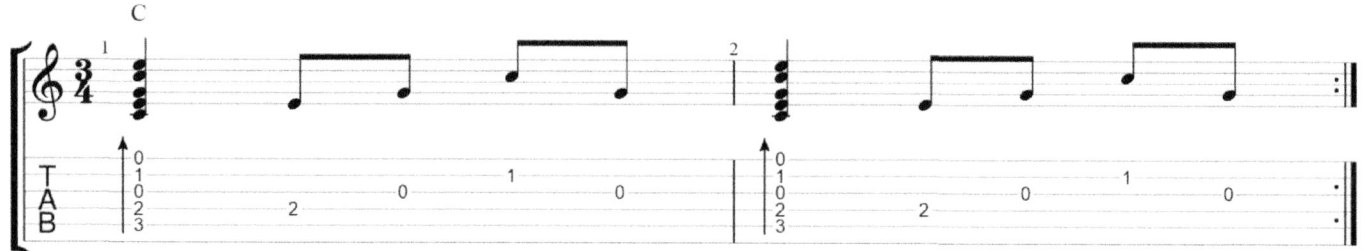

Technically speaking, arpeggios can be a lot more involved than this, but we don't want to complicate things too much at this level of guitar playing. For the sake of simplicity, any time we play the chord notes individually, even if not all of them, we'll just call it an arpeggio.

Slow / Fast Strum

In the chapter on dynamics, we looked at the technique of playing with louder and quieter strumming to highlight the first beat, or the backbeat etc. We can do something similar but instead of strumming at different levels of loudness, we strum with a varying speed of attack across the strings, i.e., strum slow or fast.

This technique doesn't seem to work so well on the beats 3 and 4 in my opinion, or at least not as often. It works very well on the first beat, especially for slower tempo songs. It also works well on the second beat but more so when combined with the bass / strum technique.

The idea is to simply strum through the strings slower than you would on a normal strum. It also should be quite subtle in most cases, just enough to stand out but not so slow that it makes the timing feel awkward.

Just to be sure we're clear, here's an exaggerated example of the differences between a slow and typical strum speed. Something like the third or fourth strum in the example below is probably about as slow as we'd want to go - any slower and it might sound more like an arpeggio played with bad timing.

Listen to the audio example to hear the differences played ranging from too slow to a normal strum.

Example 31

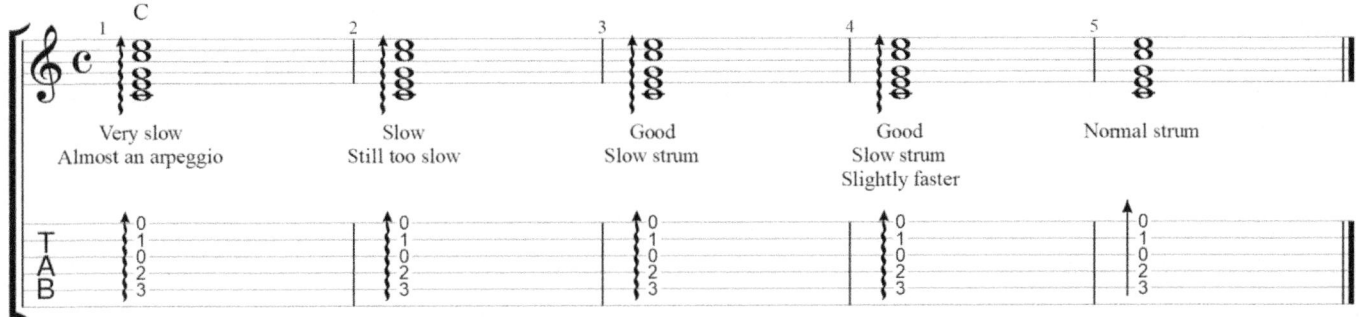

And now some practical rhythms using this technique.

Example 32 - 4/4 slow on first beats only and then normal 1/4 strums

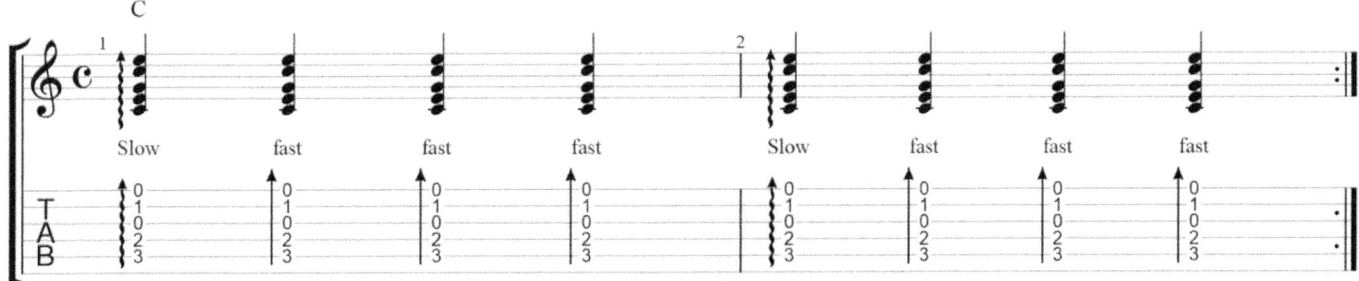

Example 33 - Bass note followed by slow strum on beat two and some 1/8th rhythms.

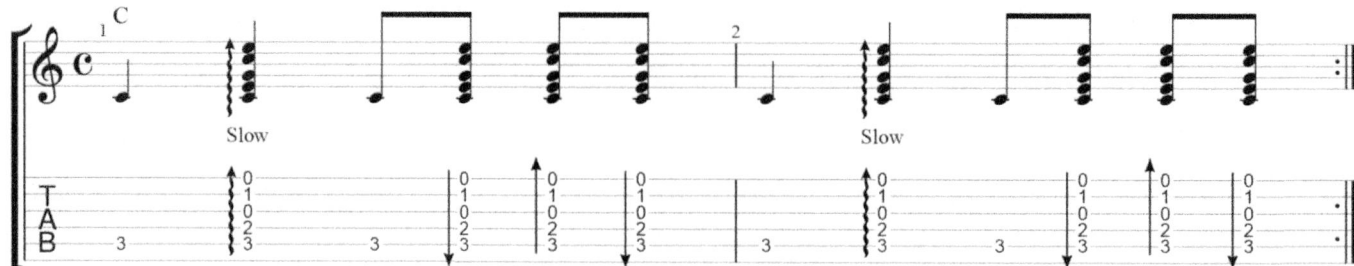

For 3/4 timing we could do the same thing, slow strum on the first beat and then two normal strums. We could also try something like the following example where we play a bass note on beat one, then a slow strum followed by a fast strum. This gives us something different for each of the three beats and sounds pretty good.

Example 34 - 3/4 bass / slow / fast

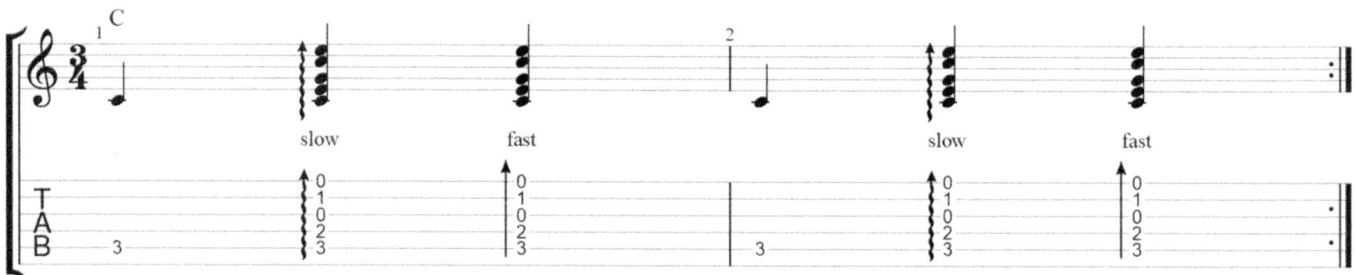

Example 35 - we can of course do the same in reverse and start from the high string as an up stroke. Even though we wouldn't normally play an upstroke on the downbeat, in this case it's the only way.

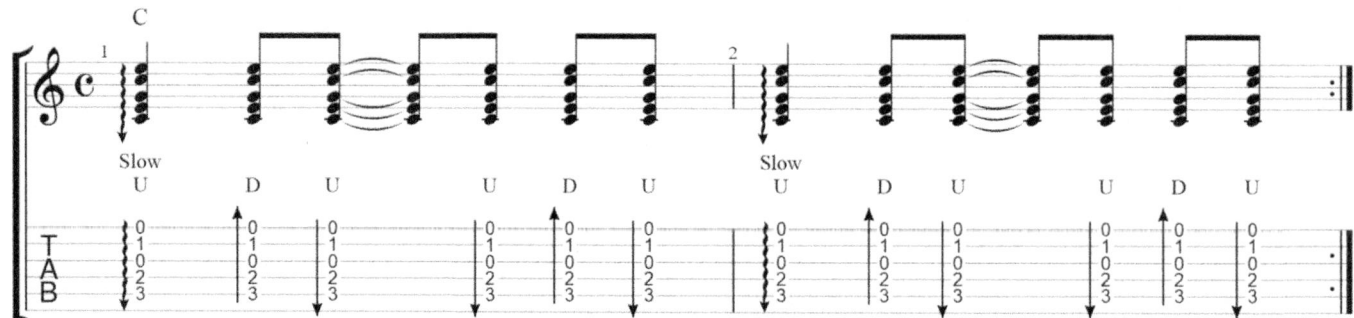

Although there is no rule, it generally sounds better if the last note of the strum ends on the beat rather than starting on the beat - which can make it sound like you are playing out of time. This takes a little bit of practice to get the timing right. Listen to the following example for a better explanation.

Example 36

The first three bars starts the strum on the beat. The next three bars try to end the strum on the beat by starting slightly earlier. It's fairly subtle but you should notice the first three bars feel like they're dragging, which, in turn, makes the following strums feel pushed.
The strums that try to end on the beat feel tighter against the metronome.

This is difficult to notate but the TAB below should give you the idea of a slow strum starting on the beat compared with one that ends on the beat.

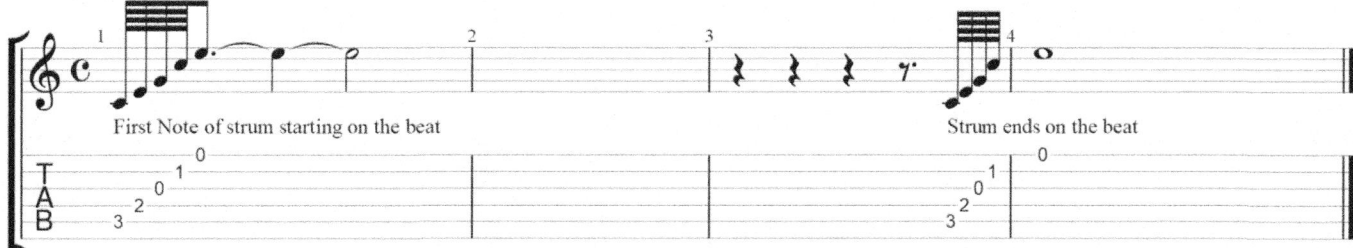

Partial Chord Strumming

We don't have to always play all of the strings in the entire chord. Just hitting a few strings of the chord here and there can give a nicer, less aggressive sound. In practice it's actually quite normal to miss a few strings while strumming, either intentionally or non-intentionally. It's not always a bad thing and can give us some dynamic variation.

In the following example, listen to the difference between a full strum and partial strum. In the first two bars I play a full strum - the next two bars I strum only the top three strings.

Example 37 - strum difference full / partial

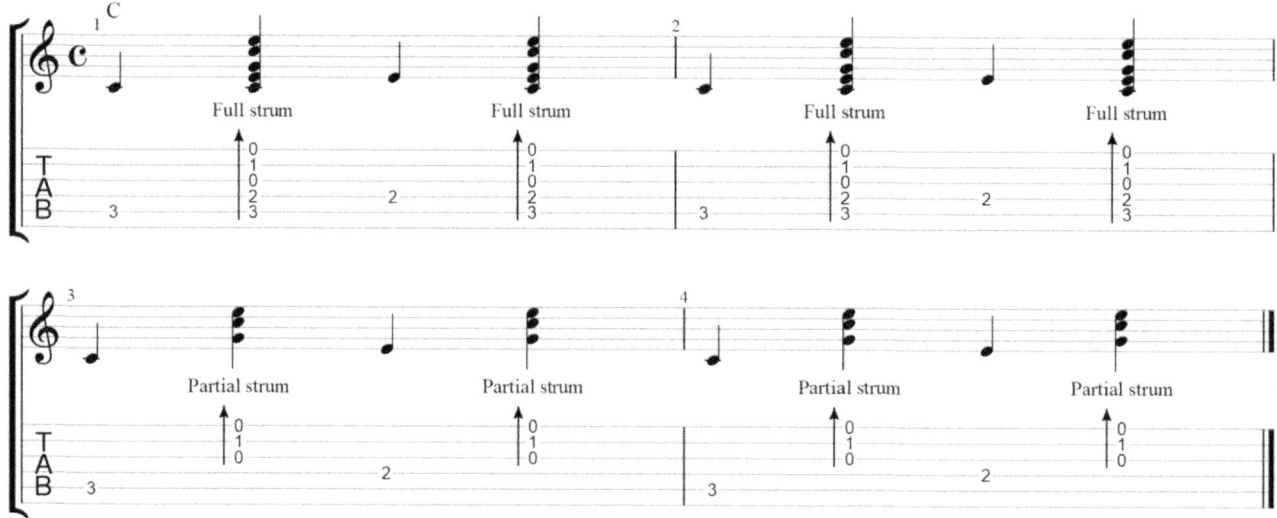

Example 38

In this example I'm doing the same thing but I'm not trying to be precise. I'm generally aiming for the lower strings on the first and third beat and the higher strings on the second and fourth beat. With each strum I'm not too bothered quite how many strings I actually hit. It still sounds OK, it's more varied than playing a full strum each time and if you are playing alongside other musicians then the untidiness of it would hardly be noticed, if at all. It can also have the positive effect of leaving some sonic space for other musicians by not having to fight against a wall of sound. There will be times when you want to play more clean and precise, but in a jam setting or live playing this will usually sound perfectly OK.

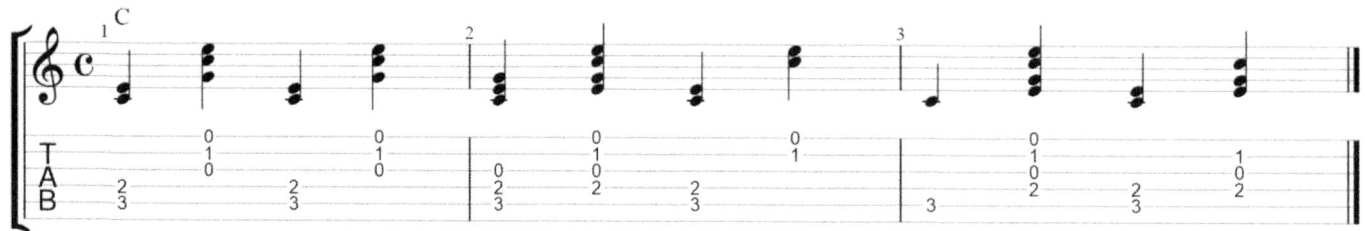

Example 39

In this example we'll do something similar. We'll play a typical DUDU-UDU Rhythm. First listen to this with full strums.

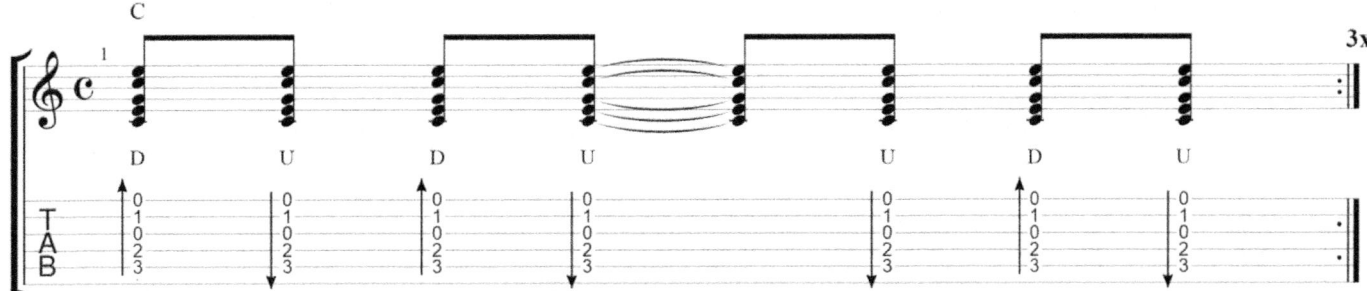

Example 40

Here we use the same rhythm but picking out certain notes and strums and playing precisely. Just follow the TAB to get the idea.

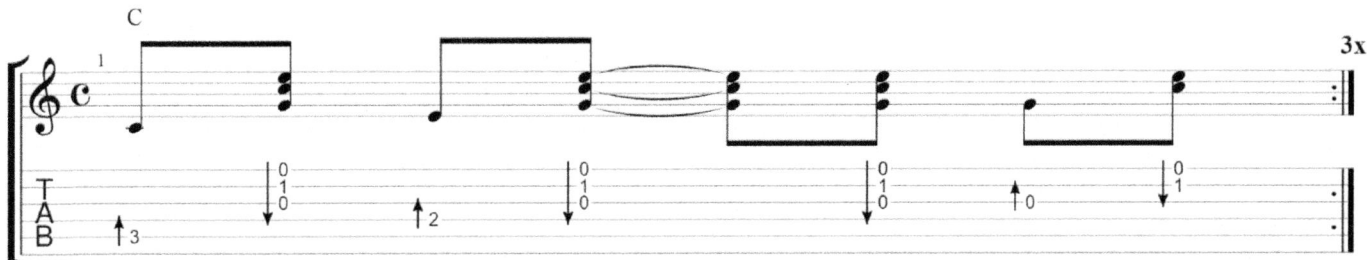

Example 41

Same again but now not trying to be quite so perfect. We still aim for playing the same thing but we're not trying quite so hard to be precise, which results in a few misses and extra hits. Still sounds not too bad though. This should only be considered "messy" if perfect is what you are aiming for, but, again, if you are playing along with others then this would probably go unnoticed.

Muting and Muted Strums

String muting is a very important technique to develop. It can take quite a lot of practice and it's also a difficult topic to demonstrate in a book, so I would advise you to watch some YouTube or other videos and just practise the technique until you get it. Either way, I'll try my best to explain things here.

Muting can be quite a diverse subject but we're only going to concentrate on the three main ones here - controlling unwanted string noise, chord mutes (stops), and the muted strum.

Unwanted strings sounding

If we play a C chord using the same shape we have so far done in this book, then generally we don't want the low E string to sound. If we hit it accidentally (or even intentionally) it's not quite so bad because it's a note that does belong to the C chord. Most of the time, however, we either stop this string ringing by gently touching it with the finger that's already playing the C note on the fifth string, or we use our thumb hooked over the fretboard to dampen the string. Same thing with the A chord, we prefer not to play the low E but it's not so bad because the A chord also has an E in it.

The D and F chords aren't so forgiving because neither have an E in them. Luckily, this string is quite easily damped with the hooked over thumb - or if you are playing the F chord as a full bar chord then there's no problem anyway. Some people will tell you that if you can't manage to hook your thumb over (or use the fingertip) then just don't play that string. This is easier said than done, especially for harder or faster rhythms, accidentally hitting these strings is still quite easily done.

The other problem with this idea is that it doesn't take into account these strings will end up ringing even if you don't touch them, just the vibrations through the guitar body can cause them to ring to a level that can become audible. Whatever way you look at it, eventually, if you want to play cleanly and have good rhythm, then muting is something you will need to be able to do.

Chord Stop / mute

We can stop a chord from sounding by lifting our fingers slightly from the strings, but not fully. In other words, hold down and strum a chord, then relax the fretting hand to release the pressure but leave your fingers still touching the strings - this will stop the strings from ringing.

This is quite easy with a bar chord that uses all six strings, something like a full F chord. Simply strum the chord and then release the pressure by lifting the fingers until the strings stop sounding - just make sure the fingers remain in contact with the strings.

For chords that use open strings, things are not always so easy. The C chord for instance will be fretting the A, D and B strings. The G and two E strings are not fretted so these will continue to sound if we played them. To stop these strings ringing we need to tilt our fingers down across the strings so that we dampen all of them, while, at the same time, the low E is dampened with the thumb.

The most difficult of them is probably the D chord. We only fret the top three highest strings which leaves the low E, A and D strings all open. I personally use my thumb hooked over to dampen all three of these strings. If you find that a struggle, but you have your pinkie finger free, then you could bring that down over the strings in front of the chord (see the images below). Both techniques can be a bit of a challenge and the only way to master this is to keep trying and practising - eventually you'll get there, just be patient.

The Muted Strum

The muted strum is when we dampen all the strings in the same way as mentioned above but then strum across them. This gives a kind of scratching / percussive sound. When used among our normal strumming this adds a lively percussive element between the strums.

We'll look at some examples of these but first a few pictures of the fretting hand to give you a better idea of muting with the thumb and / or fingers tilted.

The image on the left shows a C chord with the thumb hooked over, lightly touching the E string to stop it ringing. The image on the right shows the fingers released and tilted down to rest on the strings. None of the fingers are pressing down but just lightly resting on them. To stop a chord from ringing we need to be able to switch between the two positions quickly.

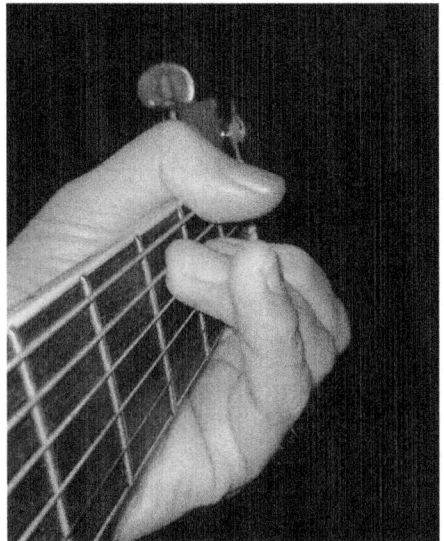 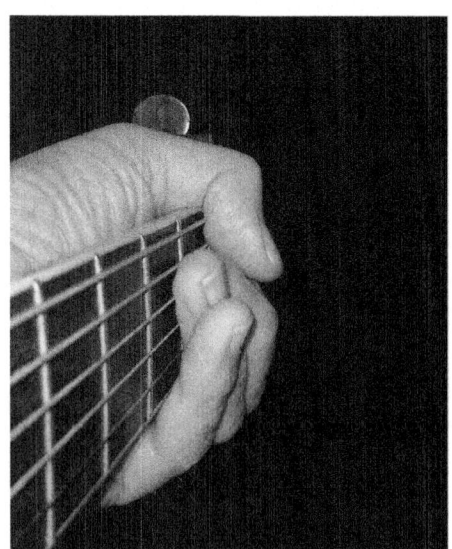

The following two images show the G chord. The left image no need to hook the thumb over because the E string (third fret) is part of the chord. The right image shows the fingers tilted down to rest on the strings. Note that even though we let go of the chord, we still keep the tips of the fingers in position so that we can switch back quickly and easily.

Below, the same again but now the D chord. In the left image I am using my thumb hooked over to mute both the E and the A strings while playing the D chord. In the right image, for the muted position, the fretted fingers are released and tilted down, but this time the tilting is caused by the need to raise my wrist up enough to bring my thumb right over and mute all three strings, E, A and D.

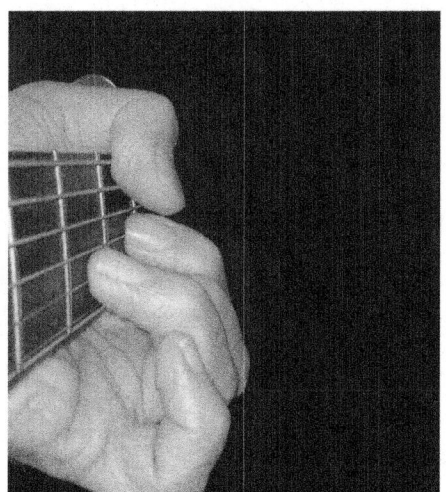 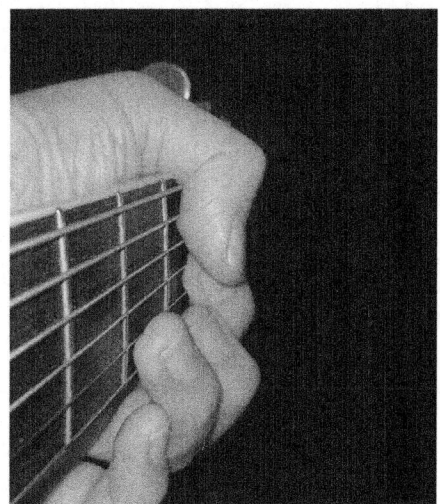

Muting all three of these strings with the thumb can be a bit tricky. Some guitarists will instead use the little (pinkie) finger, something like in the following image. Both techniques are useful so it's worth practising both of them if you can.

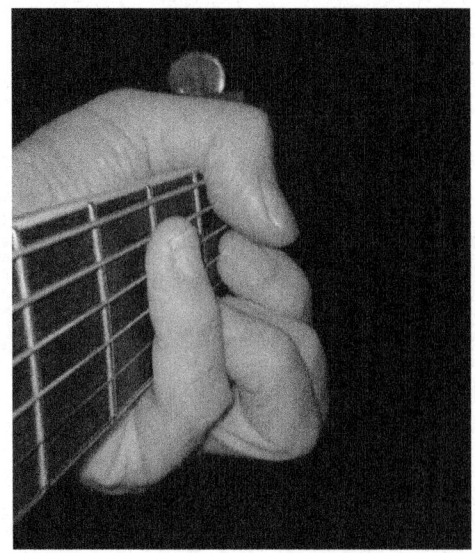

Let's now take a look at a few muting examples. If you have never tried this technique before then it might be best to start with something simple to get the feel for it. We'll just use a typical D chord like the one in the diagram below but only play the top three strings for now, the ones with our fingers on.

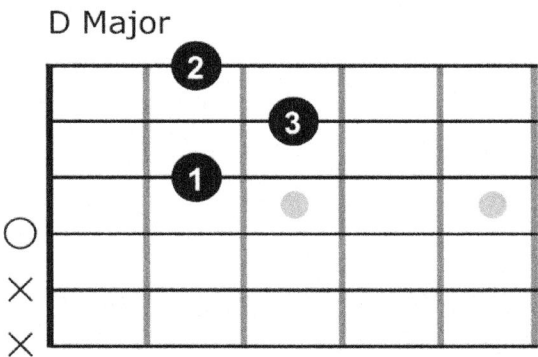

Example 42

Stopping the chord. Strum the three strings and then slightly lift the fingers. Try to make the chord stop abruptly but don't let your fingers lose contact with the strings otherwise they might create unwanted noise and start to ring again.

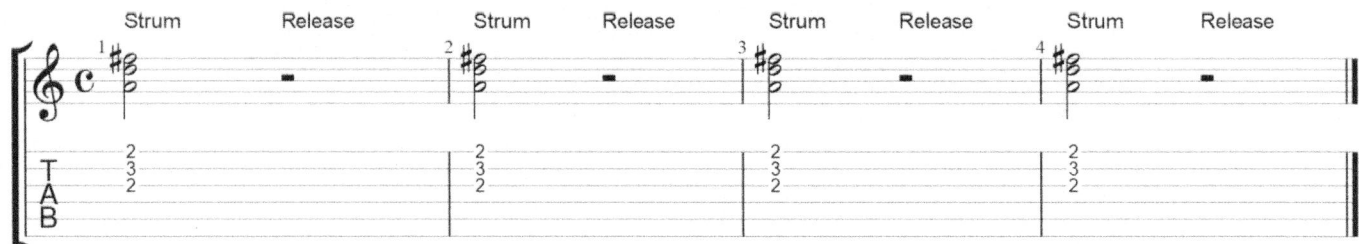

Example 43

Now we do the same thing again, only this time as soon as we release the chord, we strum again to create the dead / muted string sound. Muted strings are notated with an X in the Tab.

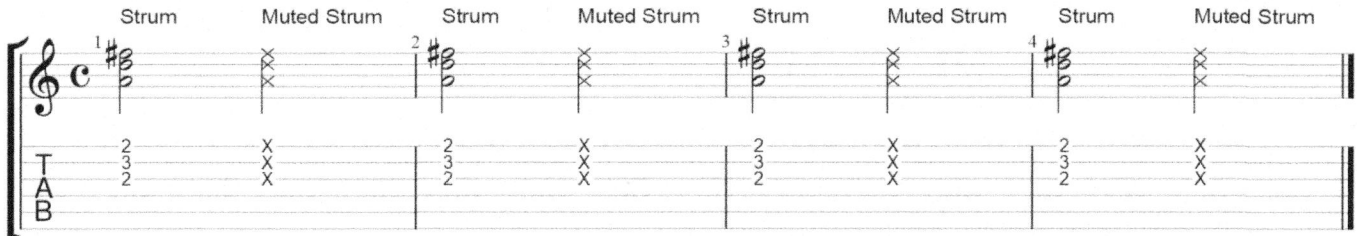

You may hear some noise from the open strings resonating even if you aren't playing them. Master this technique first before you try muting these open strings with your thumb or other fingers. The D is probably the most difficult for keeping the open strings muted so also practise with the C chord and then try as many other chords as you can as you improve the technique.

In the next few examples, we will start simple and gradually add the mutes until we build a complete rhythm pattern. Take as long as you need on each one. You might be lucky and have no problems or you might find it takes you a few weeks of practice - just stick with it. We'll use the C chord for the following examples.

Example 44

In this example we play a normal strum lasting two beats and then a quick strum / stop on beat three. Staccato is the term used to describe a note or chord that is sounded and then stopped quickly. Staccato is indicated in the notation by a small dot underneath the notes.

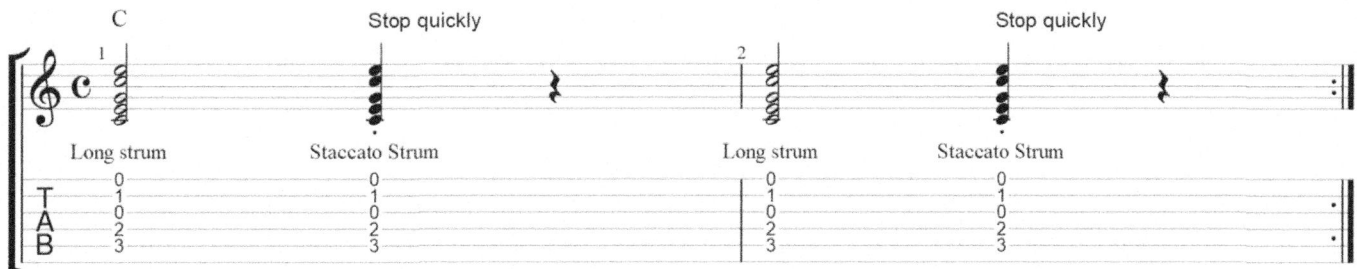

33

Example 45

In this example we do the same thing but with 1/4 notes so, in effect, it's twice the tempo. I haven't included the description text so take notice of the dot below the notes for a staccato strum.

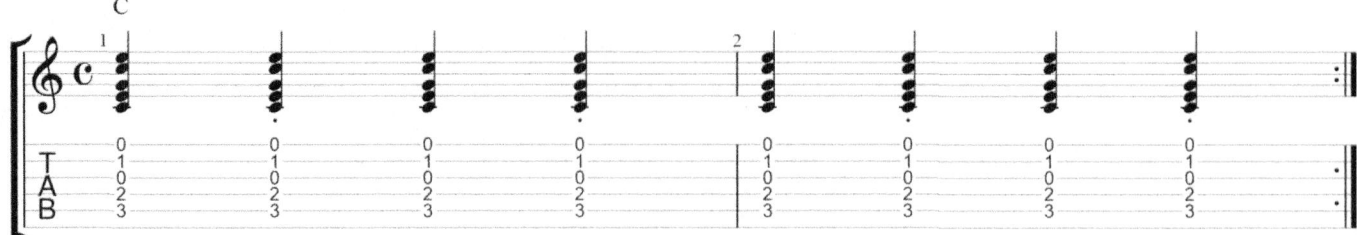

Example 46 – Now we'll add some muted strums.

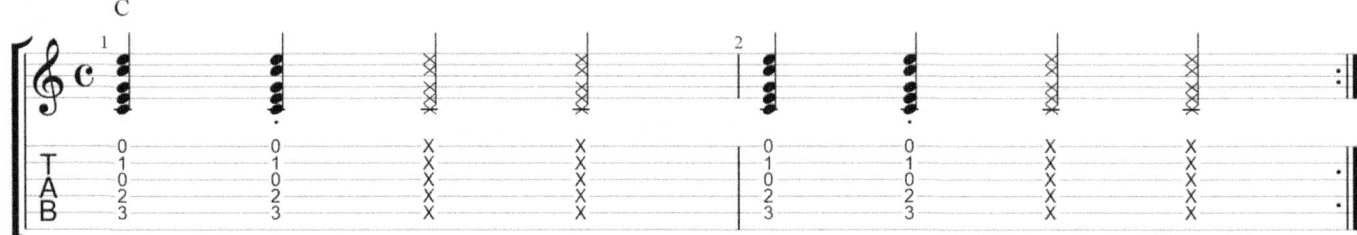

Example 47

Same again but with 1/8th note muted strums. Here the second strum only lasts for an 1/8th note and is followed immediately by a muted strum. I haven't shown this strum with a dot because it's so short that it sounds like it's played staccato anyway.

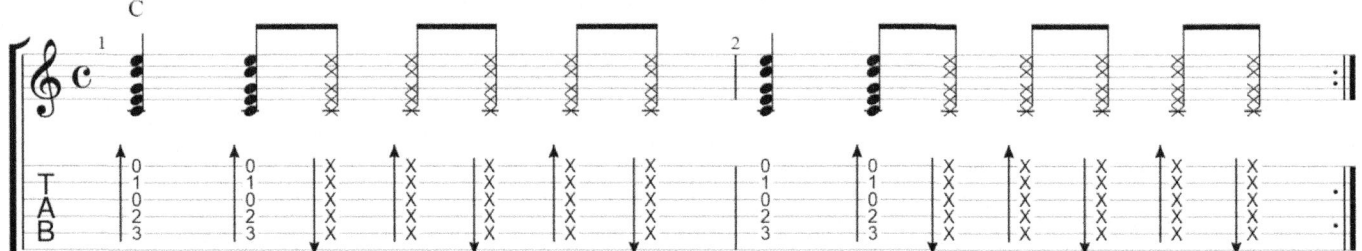

Example 48

This one is a slight variation of Example 47.

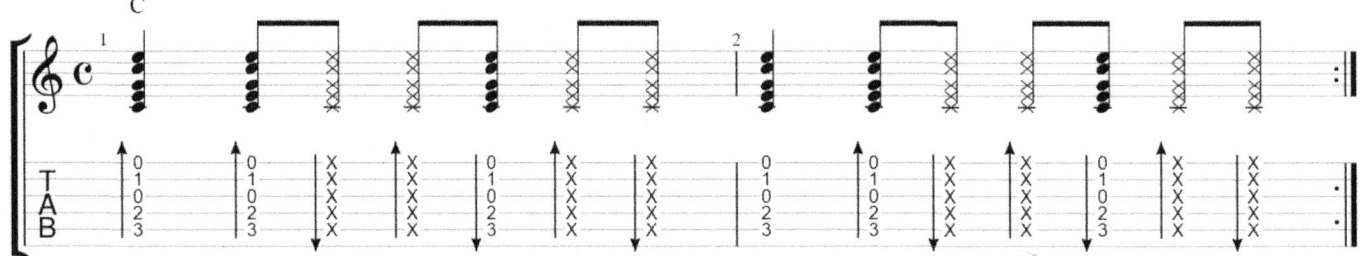

Example 49

Another slight variation. This time we won't mute the last strum in each bar, instead we'll tie it to the next. This gives it the effect of the first strum in each bar starting early.

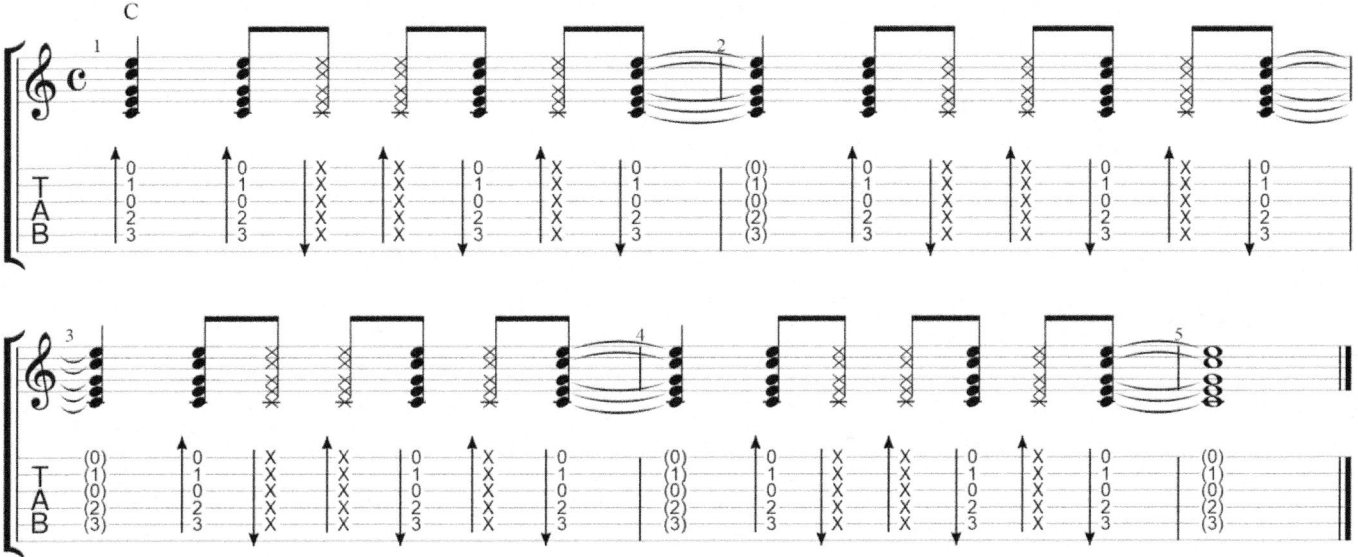

Example 50

This last one is quite a common rhythm pattern. It's just a continuous 1/8 note strumming pattern broken up by a muted strum on the 2nd and 4th beat, giving it a percussive backbeat sound.

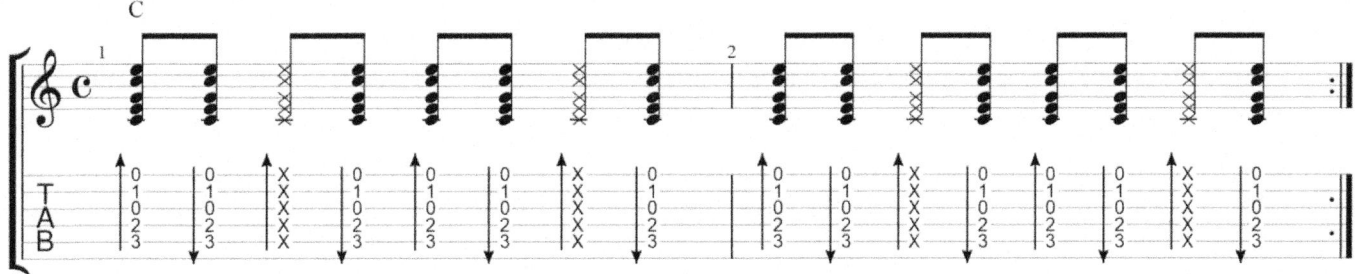

6/8 and 12/8

So far we've only looked at rhythms with a straight feel, that is a beat that's divided evenly in twos e.g., 1/4, 1/8th and 1/16th notes. We can go smaller but most of the time, 1/16ths are about as small as we need to worry about, especially for rhythm guitar playing in the styles we're talking about in this book, which is mostly dealing with 1/8th and 1/4 notes.

We can also divide a beat with odd numbers, threes, fives, sevens etc. Some of them can be very tricky and take a lot of practice but the one we can't ignore is the triplet. The good thing is we're all used to hearing it and it's not so difficult - we just need to know the different ways in which triplets are used to create various feels and timings, and know how to recognise them.

6/8 and 12/8 Time Signatures

These two time signatures can be tricky to explain the difference and sometimes even difficult to hear the difference. The tempo, the drum beat, accents, melodic phrasing, when and where the chords change ... honestly, it can be quite confusing. My advice is don't worry too much about the technical differences, as long as you know, and can hear when the chords change, then you could count in groups of three or six or even four lots of triplets. The main thing to worry about is whether or not they have a triplet feel to them and that you can recognise it.

I'm sure this might already sound confusing so let's break things down with some examples.

At the beginning of this book, I spoke about dynamics and other ways to create repeatable patterns. Without these patterns it can be almost impossible to hear the time signature. Listen to the following examples. I won't show the Tabs because this is a listening exercise so that you can understand what we mean by "feeling" the rhythm and determining what the time signature is, and whether it's a straight or triplet feel. Bear with me, I'll talk more about triplets in a little while.

All of the audio examples are available from the website shown at the end of this book (Audio Downloads)

Example 51
This is a series of guitar strums played with no variation. There is nothing we can figure out from this. It could be 3/4, 4/4, 6/8, 12/8, pretty much anything.

Example 52
Without changing anything else, here we add a kick drum. We've now made a repeatable pattern, so we have something to guide us. At this point we could safely assume it's probably 4/4 with the guitar strumming once each beat. I say probably because it could also be 1/8th notes at half the tempo. It could still possibly be 12/8. At this point I could even come up with an argument to say it's none of the above, but let's not get too pedantic - hopefully we'd all agree that listening to this makes us want to count "one two three four" starting with each kick drum. It feels like three bars of "fours".

Example 53
Here we add a ride cymbal playing eight times between each kick. It makes me want to count "One and two and three and four and". It now feels like 1/8th notes but with the strum only on the downbeat 1/4 note.

Example 54
Now we keep everything the same as above, but we'll change just the kick and nothing else. We'll put the kick on every third guitar strum. Now it sounds like 3/4 with 1/8th notes - it feels like repetitions of "one and two and three and".

Example 55
Now we'll take away the "ands" from the ride so that it's just being hit with each strum. This now feels like we want to just count repetitions of "one two three".

Remember this is just about how it feels and how it makes us want to count. Whether we are playing 1/4 or 1/8 notes, the time signature hasn't changed and to some extent neither has the feel of it. The main difference is that the 1/8th notes pretty much tells us this has a straight feel because the beats are divided evenly in two.

Example 56
Now we'll move a few things around. We'll add a crash cymbal every six strums, exchange one of the kicks for a snare and add an extra kick every sixth strum - but we'll also increase the tempo. This now feels more like 6/8. You'll probably feel like you want to count "one two three four five six", although you may still feel like you want to count two lots or "one two three" for each bar. Both are OK because you'll still have the right timing. Different songs and different grooves might have a rhythm where both types of counting feel right. There will be times when only counting "one to six" feels right, times when only "one to three" feels right, and sometimes either of them. The main thing is you'll still be dividing the bar into the right amount of beats.

Triplet Feel

With example 56 above, we get the feel of "threes" but, technically speaking, we wouldn't call it a triplet feel, it's just 6/8 with six beats to the bar. Triplets come from when we divide the time between beats into three. Like we did with 1/4 notes, if we divide the time between two 1/4 note beats by two, we get an 1/8th note. If however we divide the same two beats by three, we get 1/8th note triplets. Now instead of counting "one and two and three and four" we count "one and a two and a three and a four". Some people prefer to use the word "trip-el-et" or "straw-ber-ry" but you can use any three syllable word you like.

Example 57
Listen to this example to hear the difference. Each kick is on the 1/4 note. The side-stick starts with three bars of 1/4 notes, then straight 1/8th notes and then 1/8th note triplets. The last part with the 1/8th note triplets I am counting "one and a two and a three and a four and a". This could also be

counted with two lots of "one two three four five six". With a drum beat alone it could really be either but would become more obvious when the rest of the band and / or the singer are also playing. If the chords and melodic phrases seem to repeat in groups of six beats then it would probably be 6/8. If however you feel like the "pulse" or repetitions are in fours then it's more likely to be 12/8 because 12/8 has a feel of four lots of triplets. We'll look at 12/8 a little more in the next chapter.

This can all get a bit confusing, but the good news is we don't need to worry about it too much - the theory can be tricky stuff even for quite advanced players when we start to dig down deep. Time signatures like 3/4, 6/8 and 12/8 can all appear to seem like the same thing, it's mainly the different tempos and repetition cycles that separate them.

What matters is that we can tell the difference between a triplet feel and a straight feel. We could argue that 3/4 and 6/8 feel like triplets played slowly and that's OK as long as you feel the rhythm and can play in time then it's not a problem.

In example 57 we can hear a very distinct difference between the straight 1/8th notes and the 1/8th note triplets. This is the difference between a straight feel and a triplet feel. And more often than not, we'll probably hear it played as a shuffle rhythm - which we're going to talk about in the next chapter. Example guitar rhythms for all of the above will also be included in the song examples shown in the last chapters of this book.

The main thing to realise in all of this is that **we've used the same continuous guitar rhythm** over all of these drum variations, yet the time signature and feel has gone through quite a few changes. Without the drums we'd have no idea what the guitar is supposed to represent in terms of time and feel. Ideally the guitar rhythm should, like the drum patterns, allow us, and others, to decipher what's going on. A continuous regular strum with no variation gives us no clues, which is why we need to play with some amount of dynamic or melodic variation, enough that we can identify the musical feel just by listening.

Shuffle Rhythms

The shuffle is a rhythm with a triplet feel. You'll come across this in many genres of music. Probably the best example of the difference between a straight 1/8 rhythm and shuffle is the common blues rhythm that we've all heard countless times on the guitar. Let's take a quick listen.

Example 58

Common blues guitar rhythm. The first two bars are played straight, and the next two bars are played as a shuffle so you can hear the distinct difference.

Shuffle rhythms have a triplet feel but the second note of each triplet is either tied to the first, or isn't played. Imagine counting the triplet as "one and a two and a three and a four and a" but not saying the "and" - we would have "one _ a two _ a three _ a four _ a" - that is the shuffle feel.

Example 59

Listen to this example to hear a comparison. We'll keep it simple by playing a single E note on the bottom string. The first two bars are played with continuous 1/8th note triplets. The next two bars with a rest on each second triplet note - and then the last two bars with the first two notes of each triplet tied. This should all make sense by looking at the TAB and listening to the audio example. All three examples have a triplet feel but only the last two are considered a shuffle because the second note of each triplet is not played.

Shuffle rhythms are used in many styles of music, not just blues. When we play rhythm guitar in this or any other style, we just need to make sure we're keeping the triplet feel.

With 12/8 rhythms we have 1/4 notes divided into triplets, so it still has a 4/4 feel to it. If you look at the TAB above in Example 59, you'll see I have notated it as 4/4. Some prefer to write it as 12/8 so it will look like this:

The only real difference here is that the note groupings don't show the —3— above them, so it's just less clutter. I personally prefer to notate these styles as 4/4 - to me they just make more sense because 12/8 typically still has a 4/4 feel where the 1/4 notes are divided by triplets. Listen to the last part of example 57 - the kick is still four to the bar and is the main pulse of the beat. In short, for most styles of music, rock, pop, blues etc., 4/4 in triplets or 12/8 can be considered the same thing just notated differently.

One thing to be aware of with triplet rhythms is they can alter the Down / Up strumming patterns that you might be used to. Typically, we use down-strums on the even beats and up-strums on the odd. With triplet patterns, things are a bit different. Here's a few examples.

Example 60

All 1/8th triplets, consistent up down. Here we start each bar with a down strum and then each beat alternates between up and down, this forces each 1/4 note beat to start on an alternate down / up.

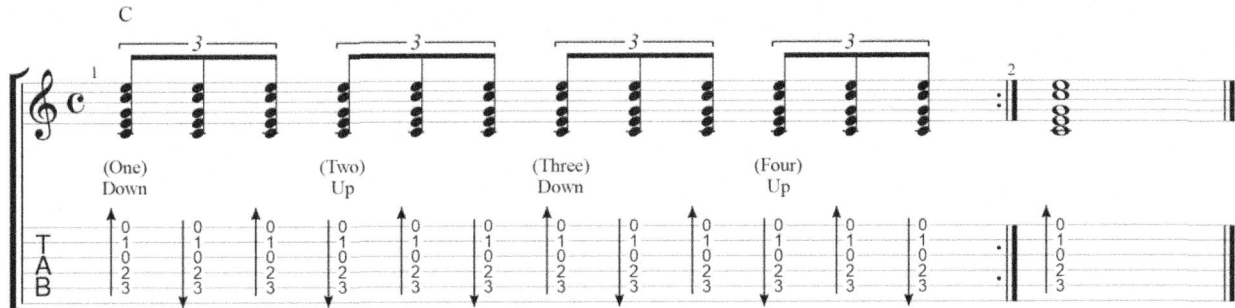

Example 61

At slow tempos we might decide to play all down strums throughout, which is what I'm doing in the first two bars of this example. In bars three and four I'm playing Down Up Down Up throughout. This feels quite natural and works just as well at slow tempos, but at faster tempos it becomes more of a necessity.

Example 62

This rhythm starts with a down strum but each subsequent bar starts with an up strum. It doesn't follow a strict down / up pattern and start each bar with a down strum like we normally would. We can try to alter the strumming pattern so that every bar starts with a down strum but this might end up making the flow of things feel unnatural, or difficult, depending on the tempo. These types of things are OK and sometimes unavoidable, so just be sure to practise and get used to them.

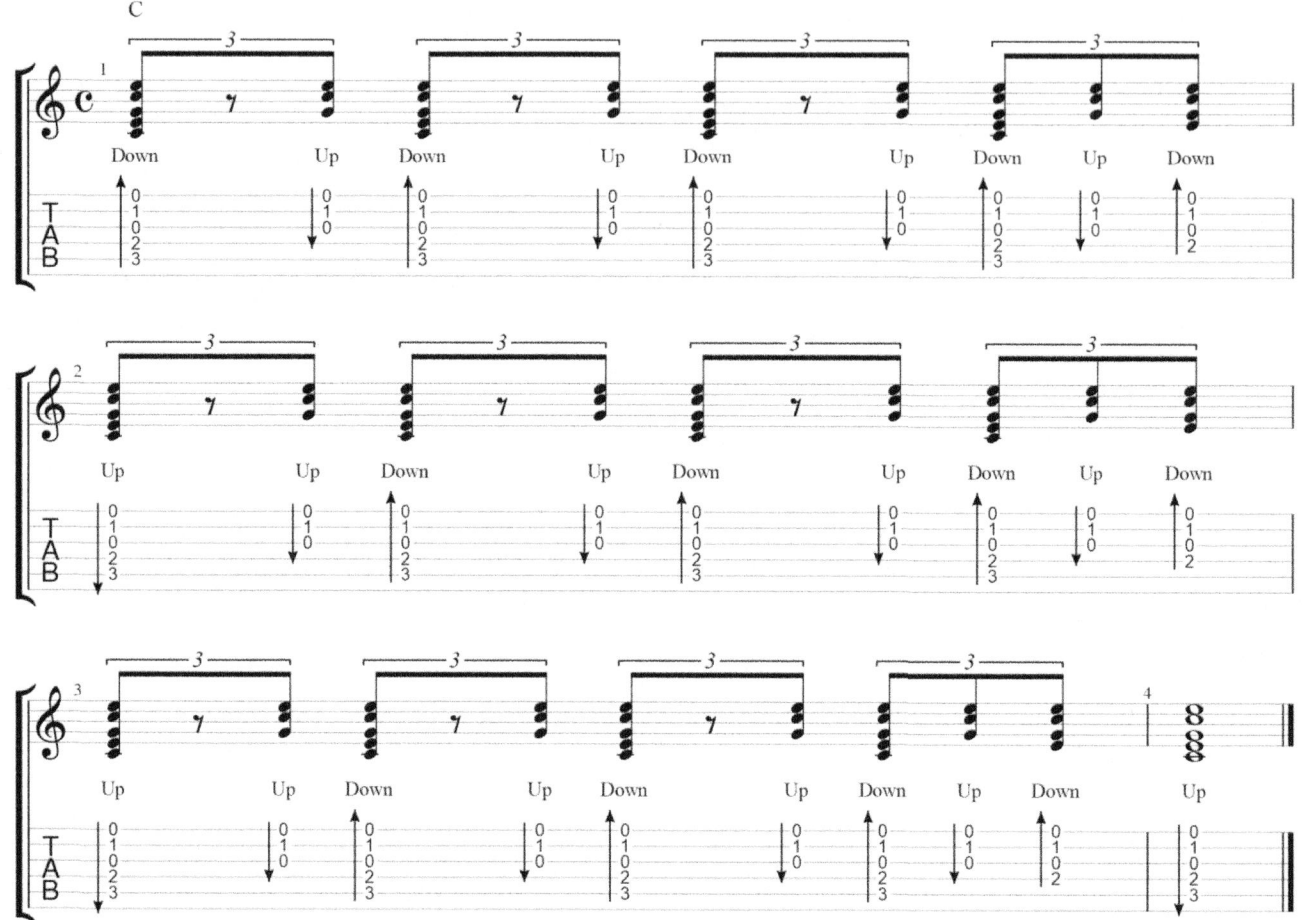

Shuffle and Triplet feel notation and TAB

In the examples so far we have looked at the difference between how we write or notate the music using either a 12/8 time signature or 4/4 with the triplets shown using a —3— above the beams. There is also another type of notation you will come across which is the Triplet Feel marking. Take a look at the TAB below. Each of the three bars are all played exactly the same.

In bar one, the first two notes of each triplet are tied. Simply put this means play the first note and let it continue to sound through to the next without playing (picking) it again. In other words, if two tied notes are the of the same value, then the note duration is doubled. Just like an 1/4 note is twice the length of an 1/8th note.

With that in mind it should make sense that the way this is notated in bar two should be the same thing as bar 1 - we're just replacing the two tied 1/8 note triplets with a 1/4 note triplet.

Writing notation is all about keeping things less cluttered where possible, so now we can use the triplet marking. Take a look at the marking above the start of bar 3 - it shows that two 1/8th notes should equal a 1/4 and 1/8th triplet, which is exactly what we have in bar two.
All this means is that we can now write cleaner, ordinary 1/8th notes in the Tablature, but it should be played with a shuffle feel. You may sometimes see this written as "triplet feel", "swing feel" or just the note markings. Either way we play it just like the shuffle and count "One a two a three a four a".

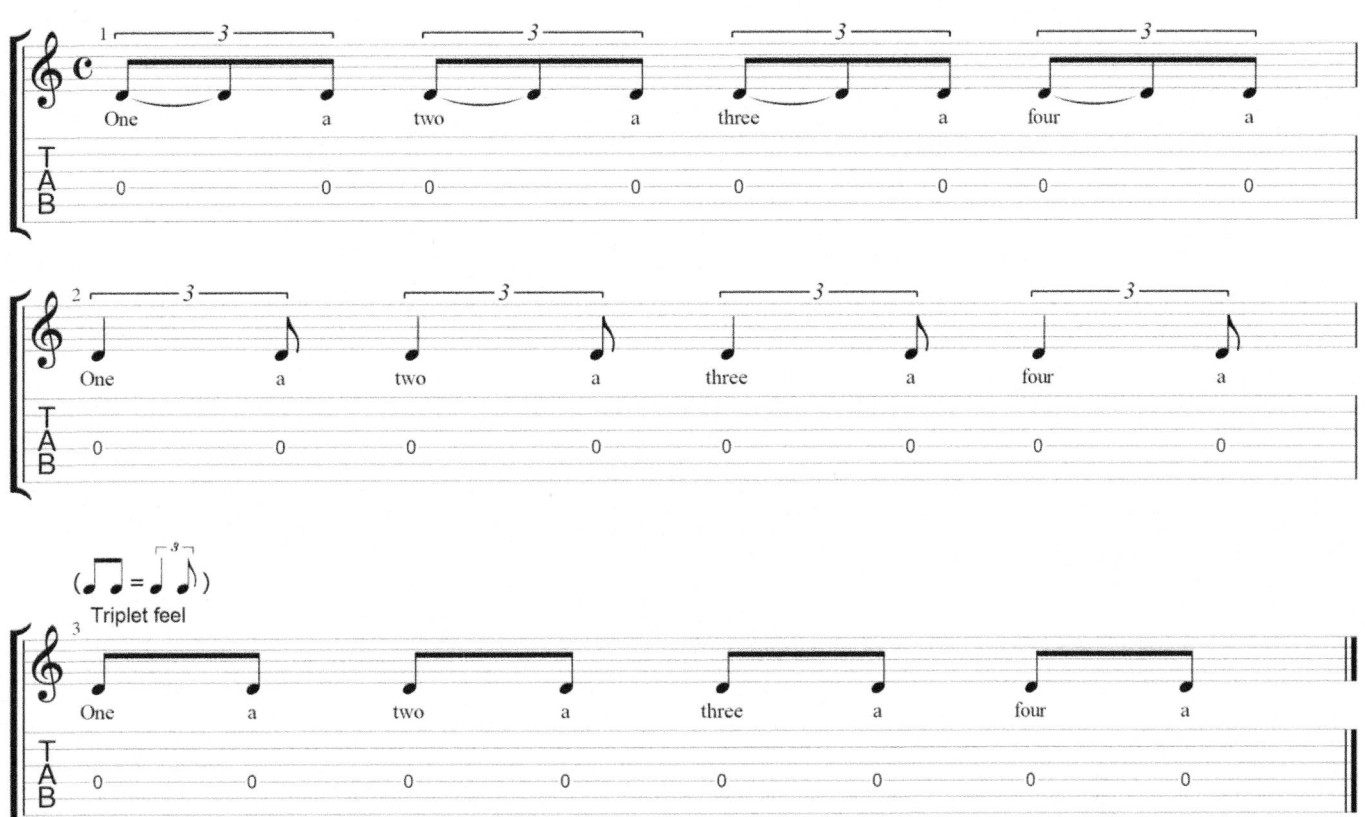

Changing Chords - Keeping the Flow

All of the examples so far have mostly only used the C chord to describe and explain rhythms and timings etc. This is a good way to practice strumming patterns but obviously at some point we need to think about the chord changes. As this book is for the advanced beginner, it assumes you can already play the common open chords without too much struggle. The next level to this is being able to transition from one chord to another, cleanly.

Smooth flowing chord changes

Some chord changes are easier than others, for example going from C to Am we only need to move one finger and it's easy to do so quickly and cleanly. Others like, let's say, E to A, depending on what fingers you use, will most likely require you to lift each finger from the strings, even if only for a fraction of a second.

No matter how hard you try, when you release your fingers from the strings, they are going to create some string noise. What we need to do is minimise this so that it becomes unnoticeable as much as possible. If you are playing in a rhythm section of a band, then you might get away with more than if you are playing unaccompanied.

Firstly, the main thing we need to avoid (unless intended) is lifting our fingers too early, causing us to strum the open strings. This might be more likely to happen on faster songs where the last strum is an 1/8th note before the change, something like in the example below.

Example 63 - Change from E to A with strumming all open strings on the last beat.

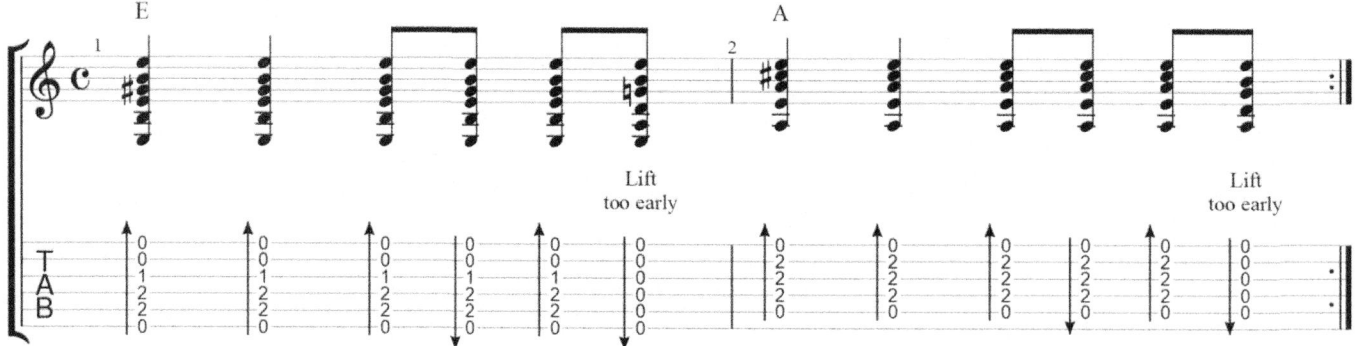

We need to hold the previous chord down as long as possible so that we don't actually strum the open strings (unless intended). They will still ring out to some extent by just lifting the fingers off from the strings but nowhere as noticeable as if you actually strum during this moment. Keep the transition as short as possible so that the duration of these open strings ringing is kept to a minimum. Doing so will make this barely noticeable, if at all.

The other thing we want to do is keep our fingers down on the strings with common chord tones.

This way we'll have fewer unwanted open strings ringing out. For example, take a look at the difference between the C and F chords in the diagram below. Our first and third fingers are common to both chords. Practise keeping these two fingers pressed down on the strings and only moving the finger from the fourth to third string, while at the same time just dropping the fourth finger down onto the fourth string.

This will create a very smooth transition, leaving only the open first string as a problem. What we want to do here is tilt the first finger so that it bars across the first two strings, but while keeping the pressure down on the second string. This is quite tricky to do cleanly and will take practice to do the whole things smoothly.

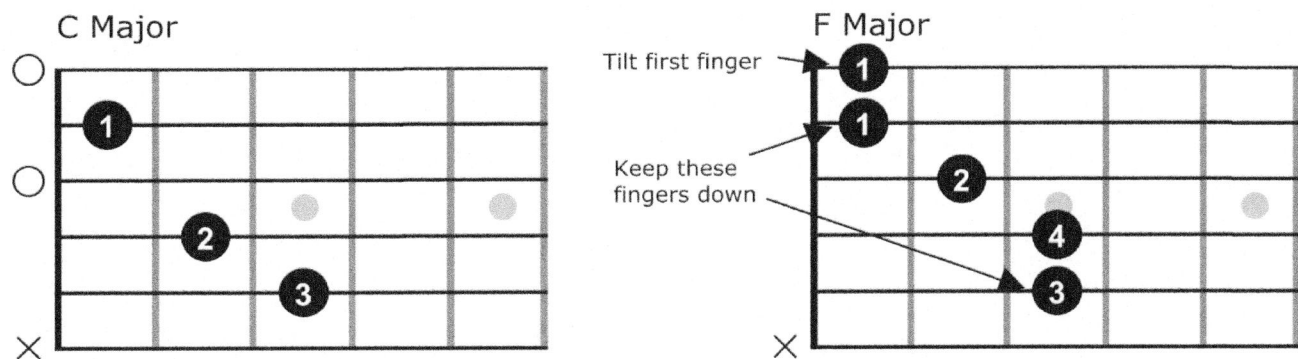

We can use a few tricks in this situation which can help. The first one might happen naturally. If the time between strums is very short then you might find that as you tilt your finger, you can't do it quickly enough and it causes the first string to mute. This is OK because it will simply stop it from ringing open. This gives you time to correct it on the following strum.

If you find this happens easily without effort, then there's nothing necessarily wrong with doing this intentionally. You might even find this works as a nice effect by doing something like keeping it muted for the first half bar, and then fretting it on the second half, making it a melodic effect. Just listen to what you are playing and decide for yourself if it fits.

The other thing you can try on the awkward changes is to strum only half the strings or even just the bass note on the first beat - like we did in chapters "bass and strum" and "partial chord strumming".

Another option which will generally work in fast tempo strumming is to just very lightly play the last strum before the change and aim for just the first one or two strings. This can work OK as long as the duration is short. Just experiment and listen, or better still record yourself to hear what it sounds like. If you are playing alongside other musicians and the song isn't too slow then this will likely go unnoticed - but of course, still keep practising in the meantime!

Example 64 - chord change with hitting first and second strings lightly.

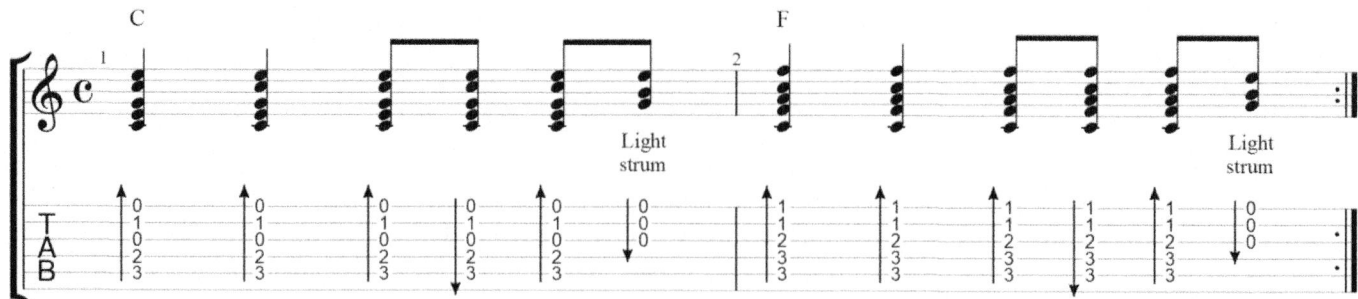

Backing Tracks and Chords

Now it's time to put all of this into practice. I have provided a variety of backing tracks and examples which you can download from the website - details are in the *Audio Downloads* chapter at the end of this book. You can listen to the song examples with the backing track or just guitar on its own.

There are backing tracks in 3/4, 4/4, 6/8 and 12/8 in a variety of styles and keys using mostly all open chords and different rhythm / strumming patterns so there is plenty to practise with. Feel free to experiment and try out some variations of your own, the strumming patterns provided are just ideas, but many other variations will work just as well.

Each example has two strumming variations. One on the first half and another on the second half.

The example tracks shown in this book use all open chords apart from F major. The backing tracks are also available on the website downloads page in a variety of keys, some of which will use the closed position chord Bm, so I have included it in the diagrams below.

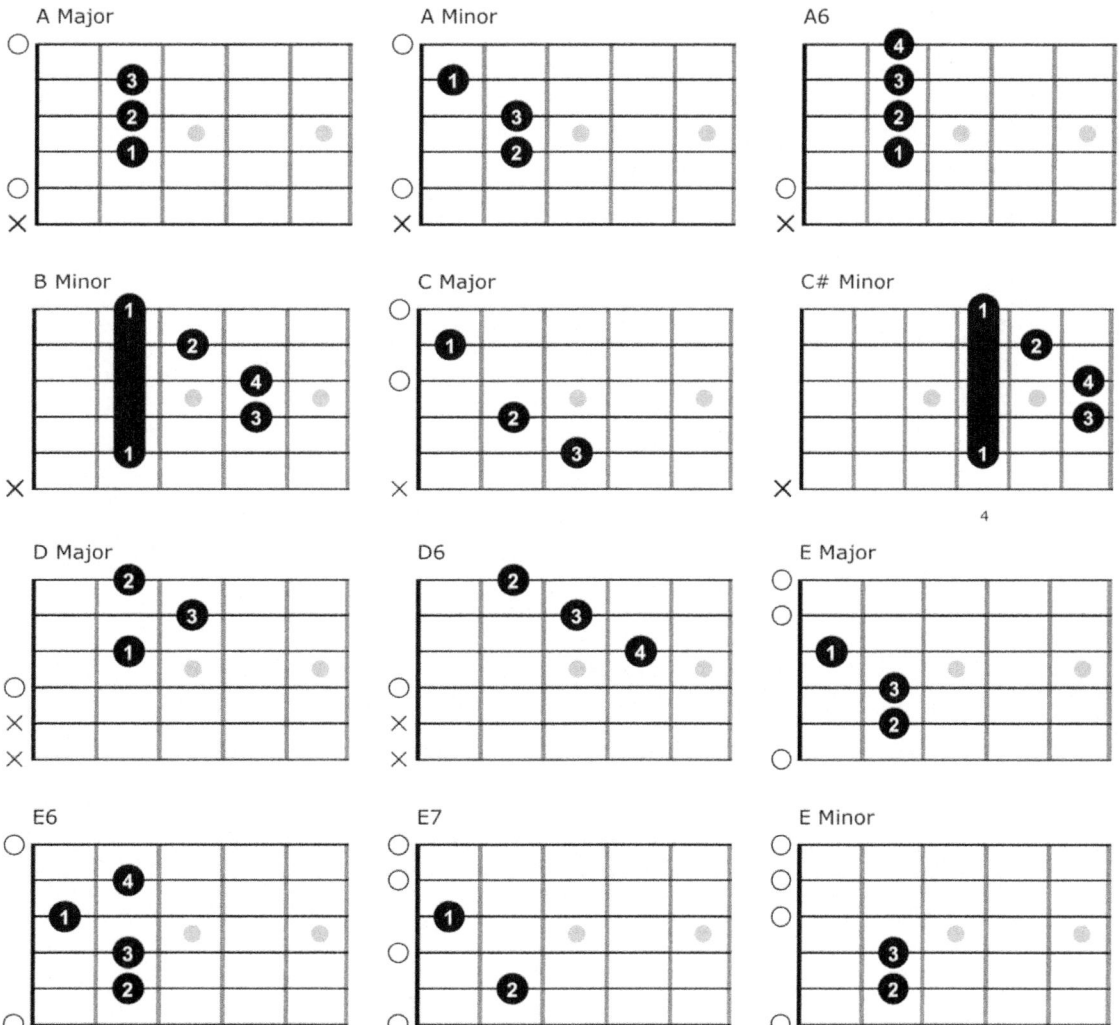

Example Song 1

Medium tempo country pop 4/4 in the key of C.

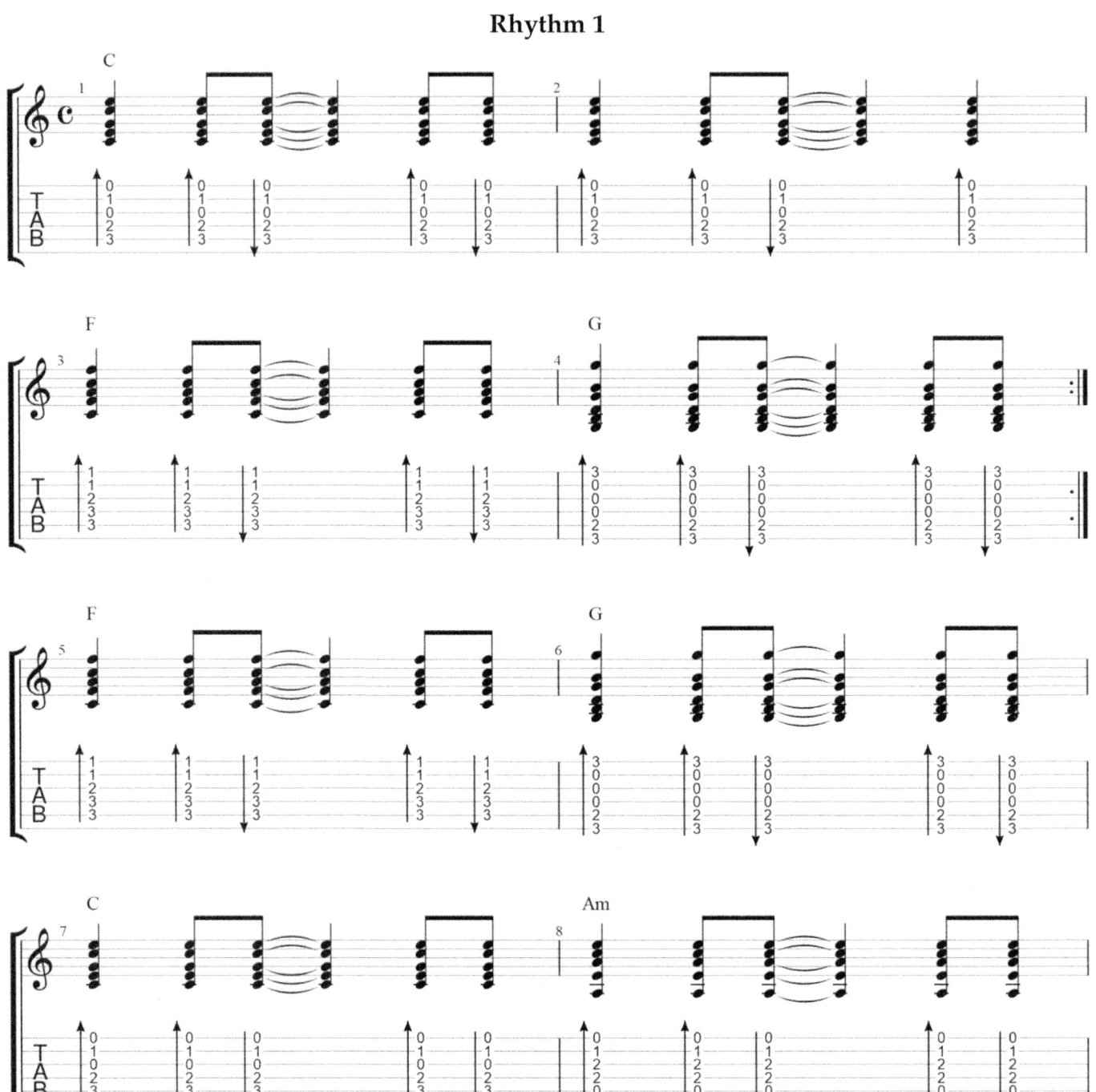

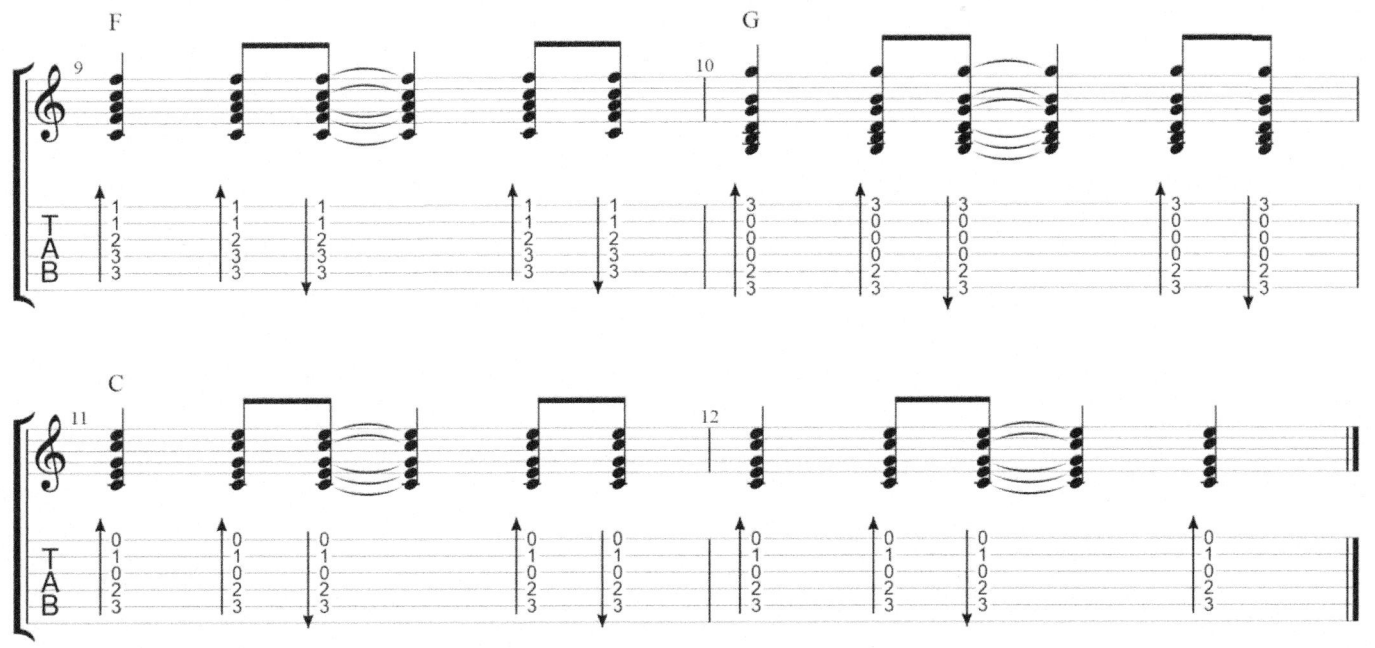

Rhythm 2

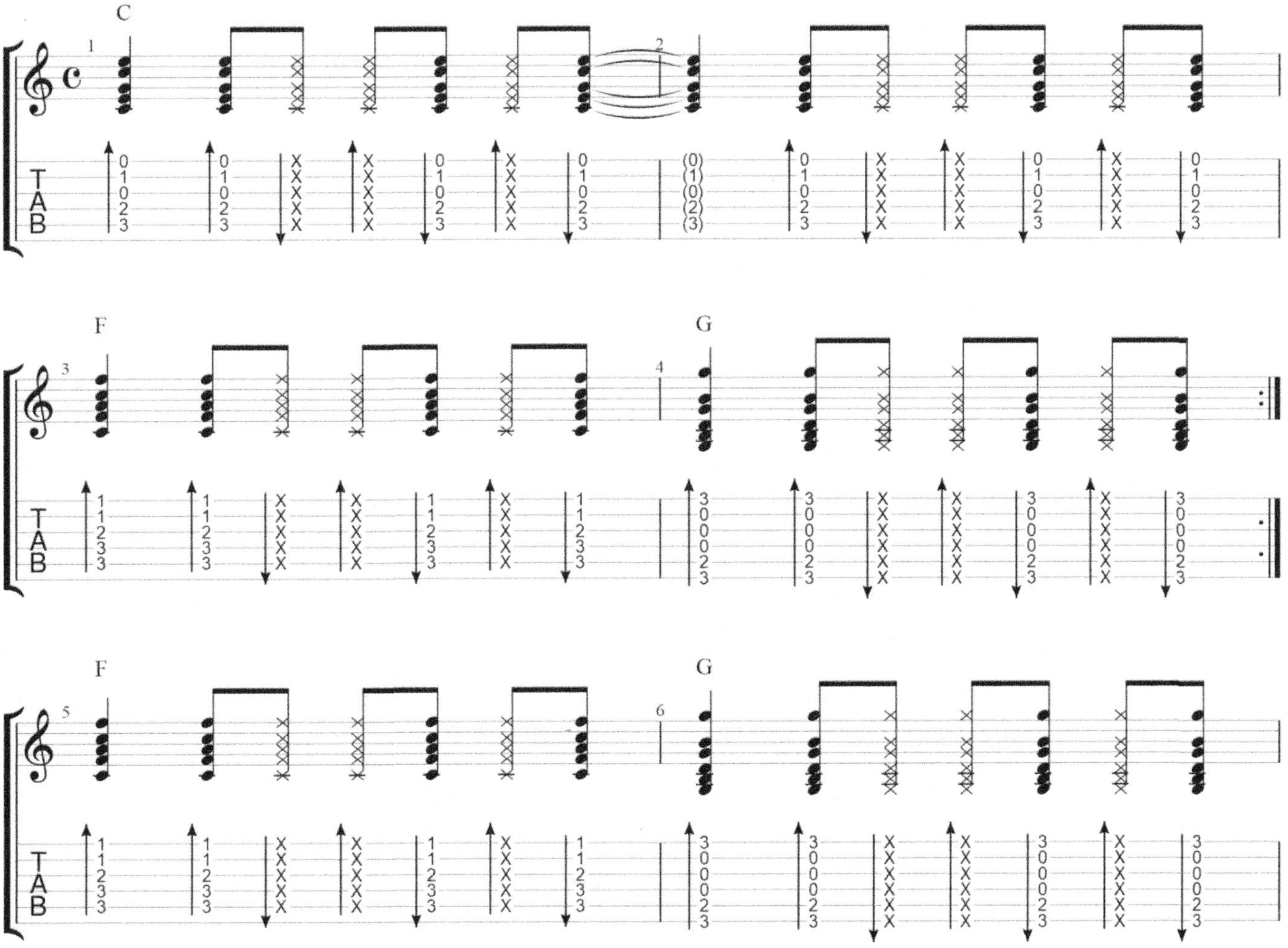

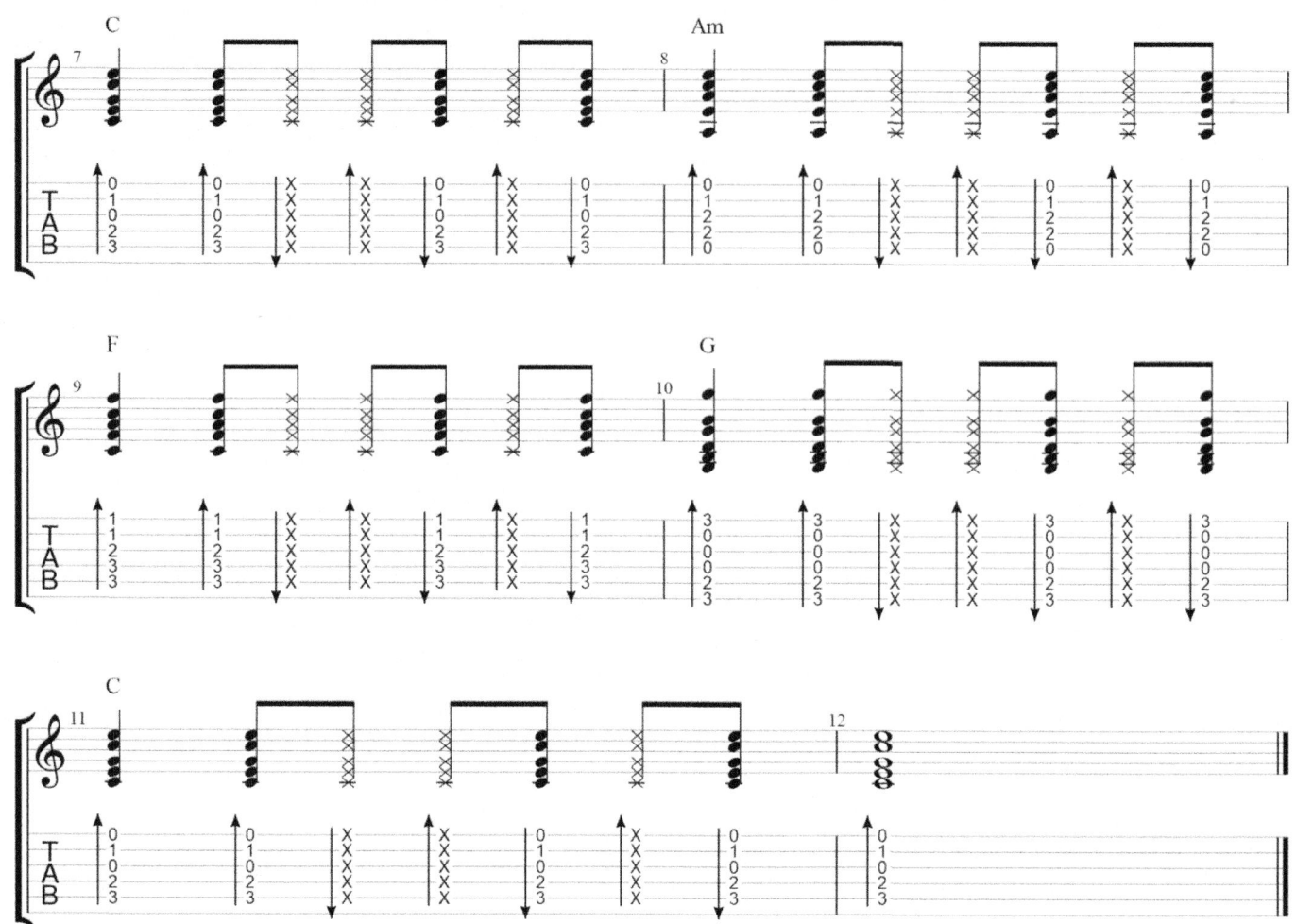

Example Song 2

Medium tempo folk pop 4/4 in the key of G with a triplet feel.

Rhythm 1

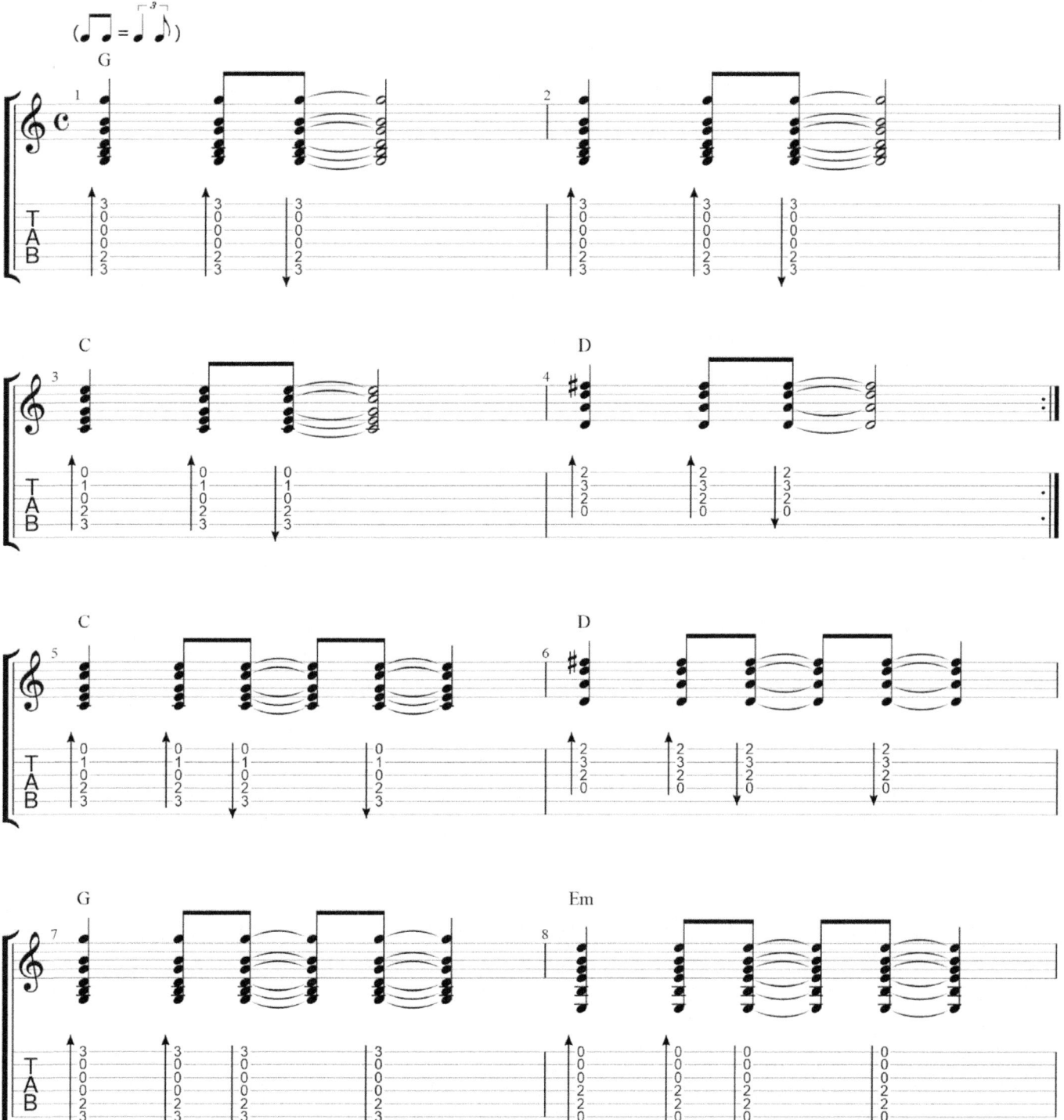

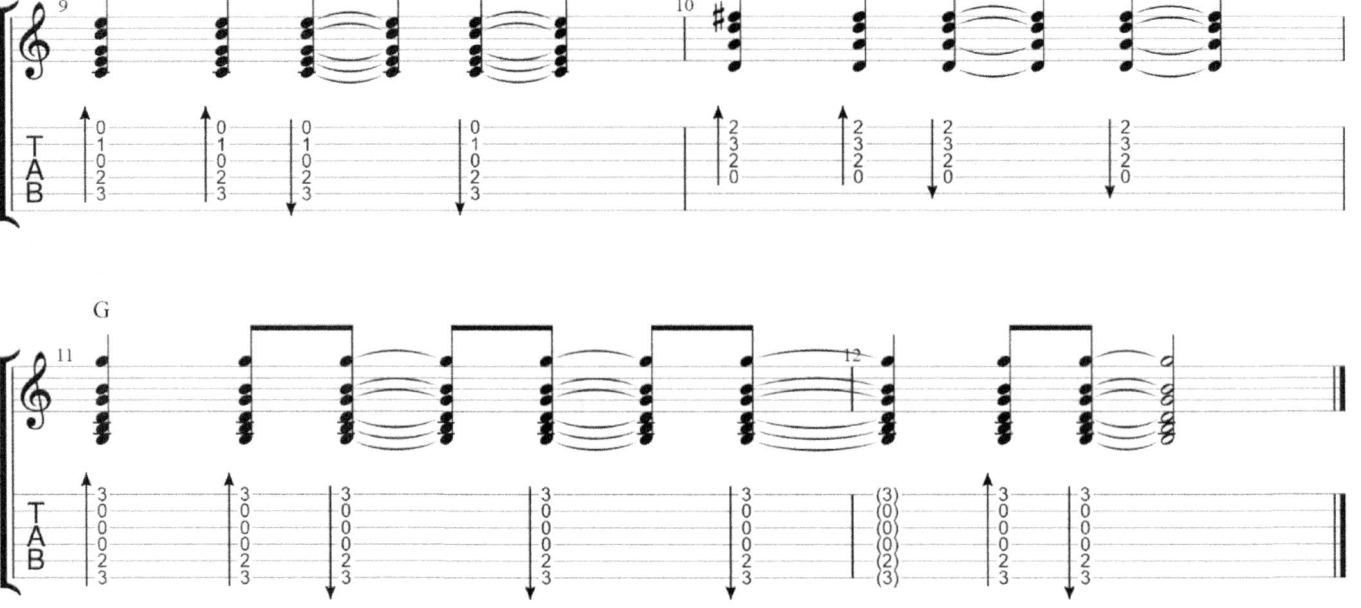

Rhythm 2
With muted strums

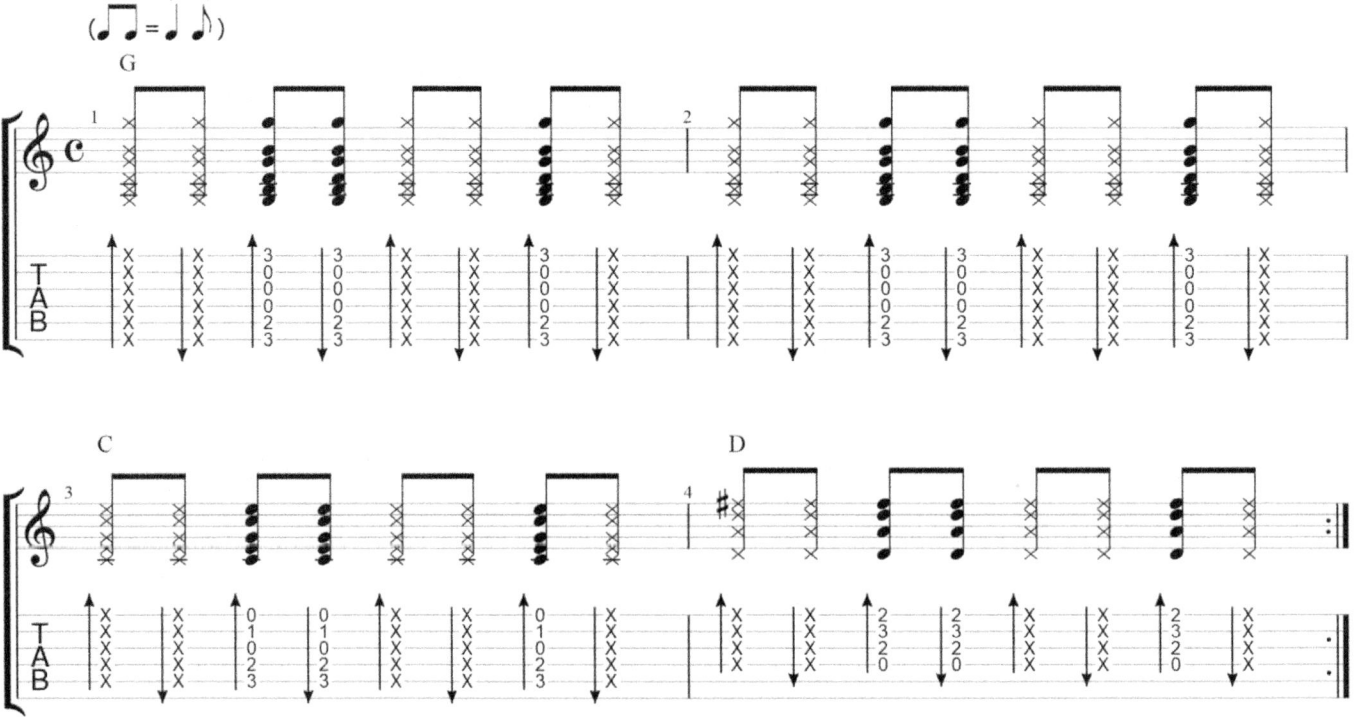

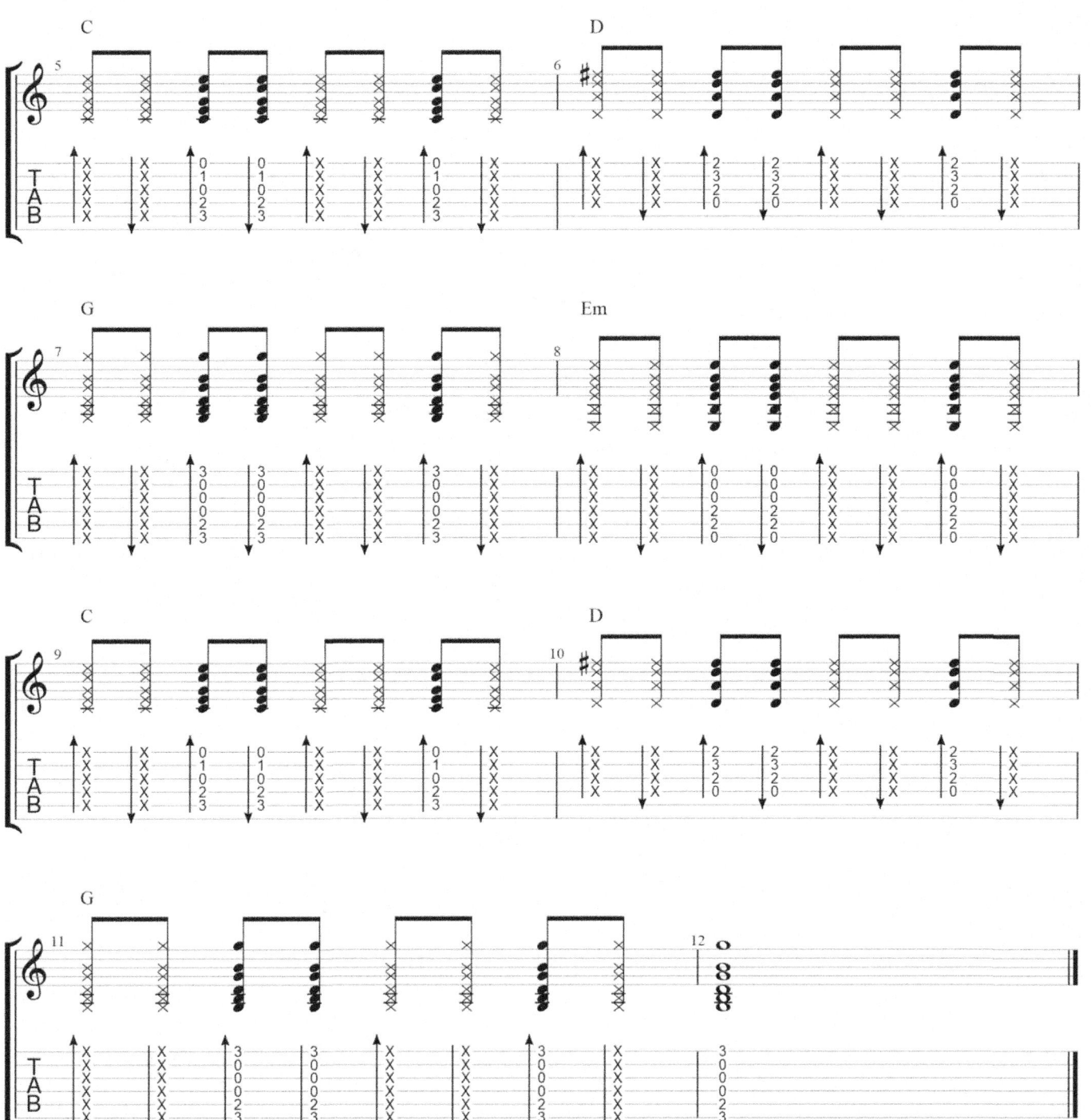

Example Song 3

Medium tempo Country Honky Tonk. 4/4 in the key of C with straight feel.

Rhythm 1

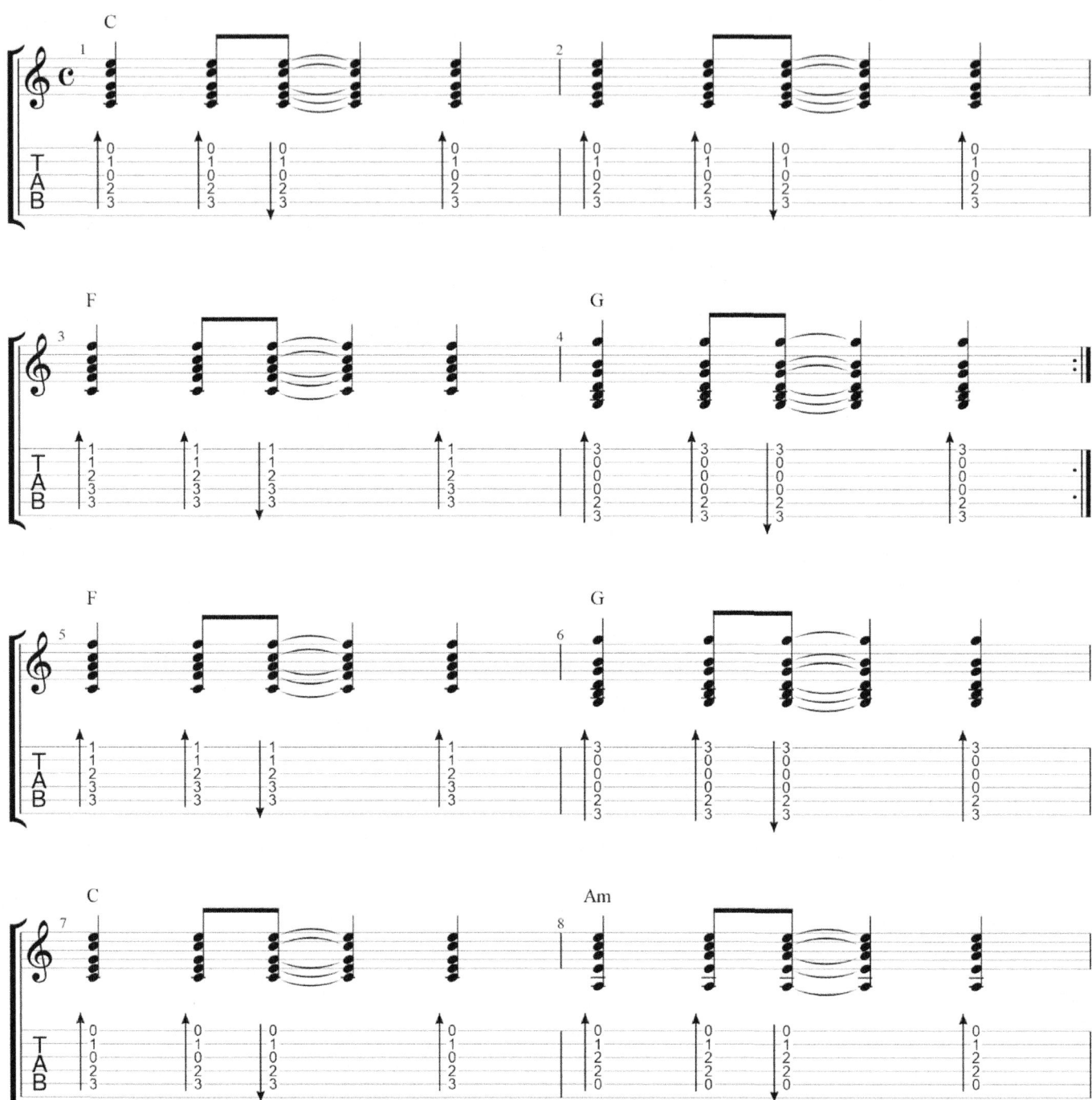

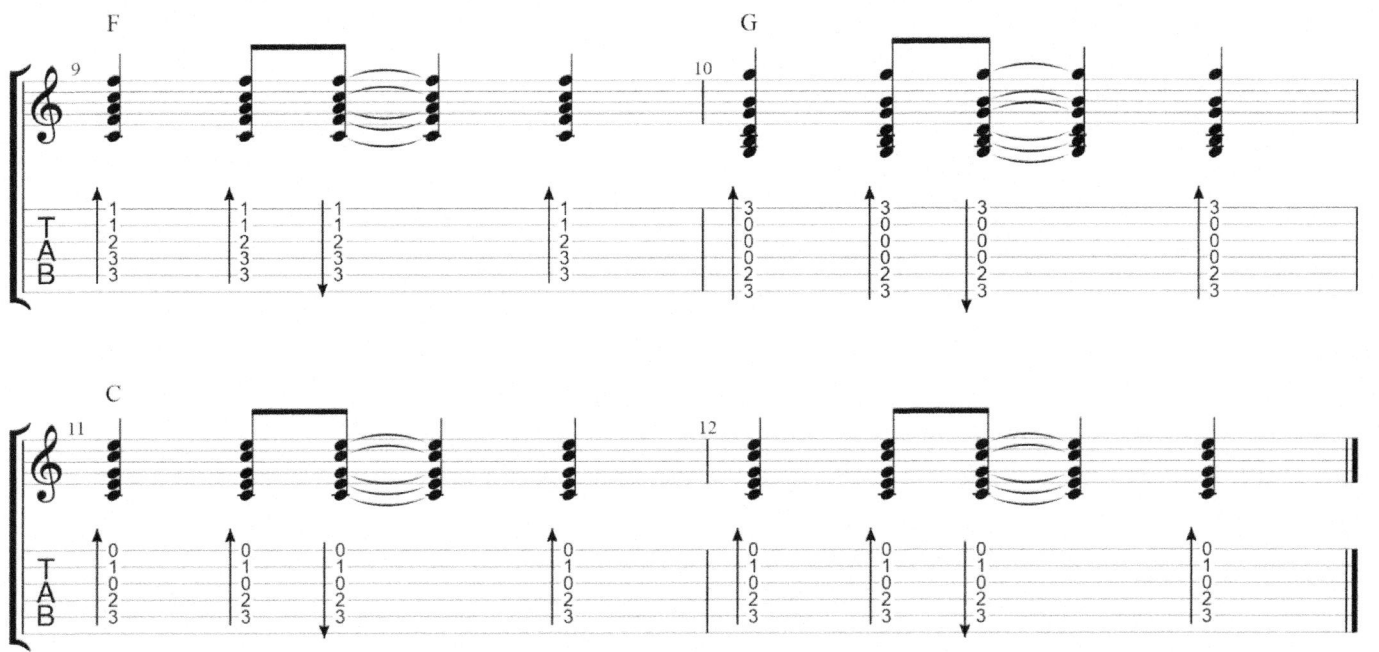

Rhythm 2
With muted strums

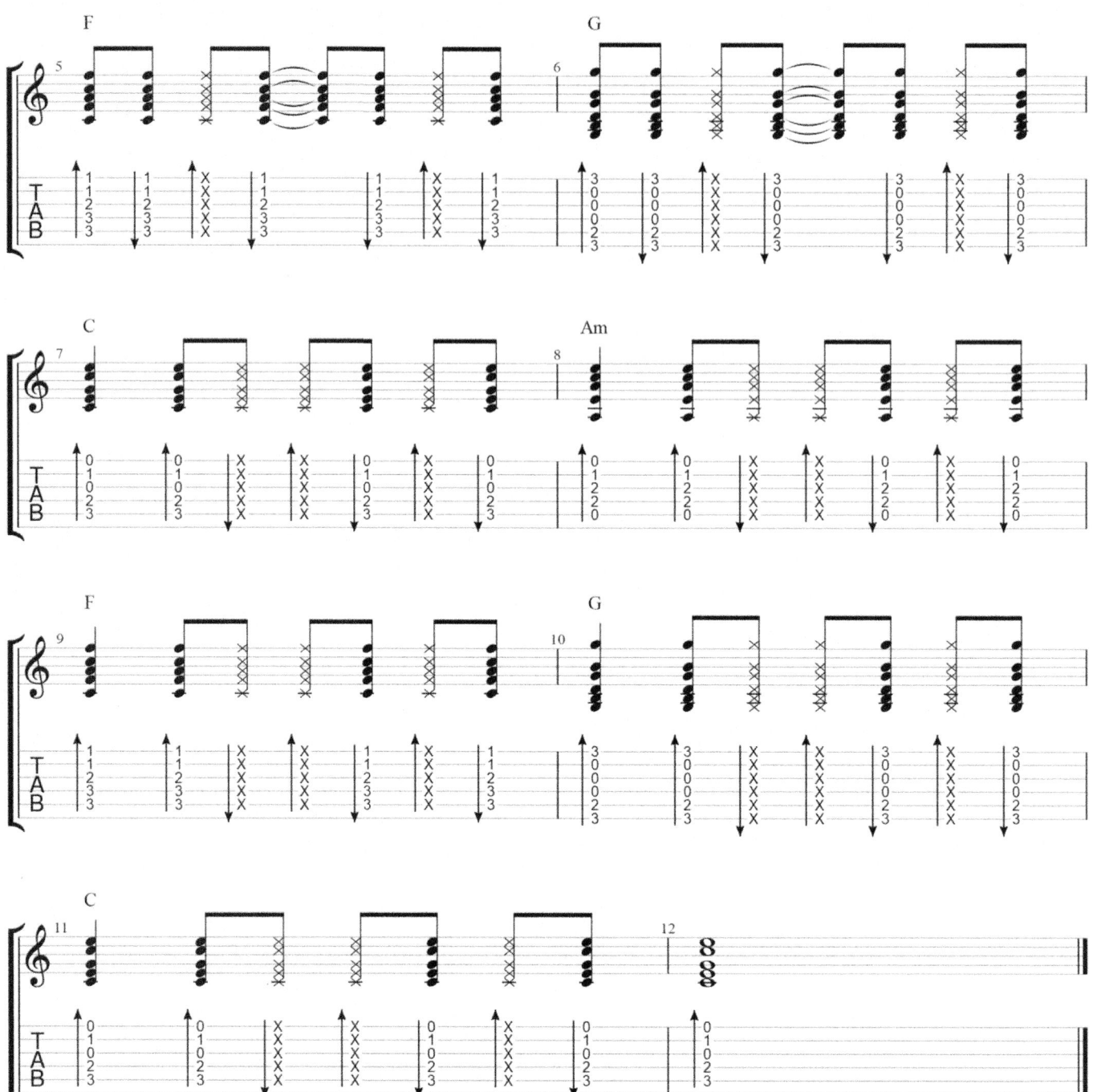

Example Song 4

Medium Country Ballad. 4/4 in the key of C with straight feel.

Rhythm 1

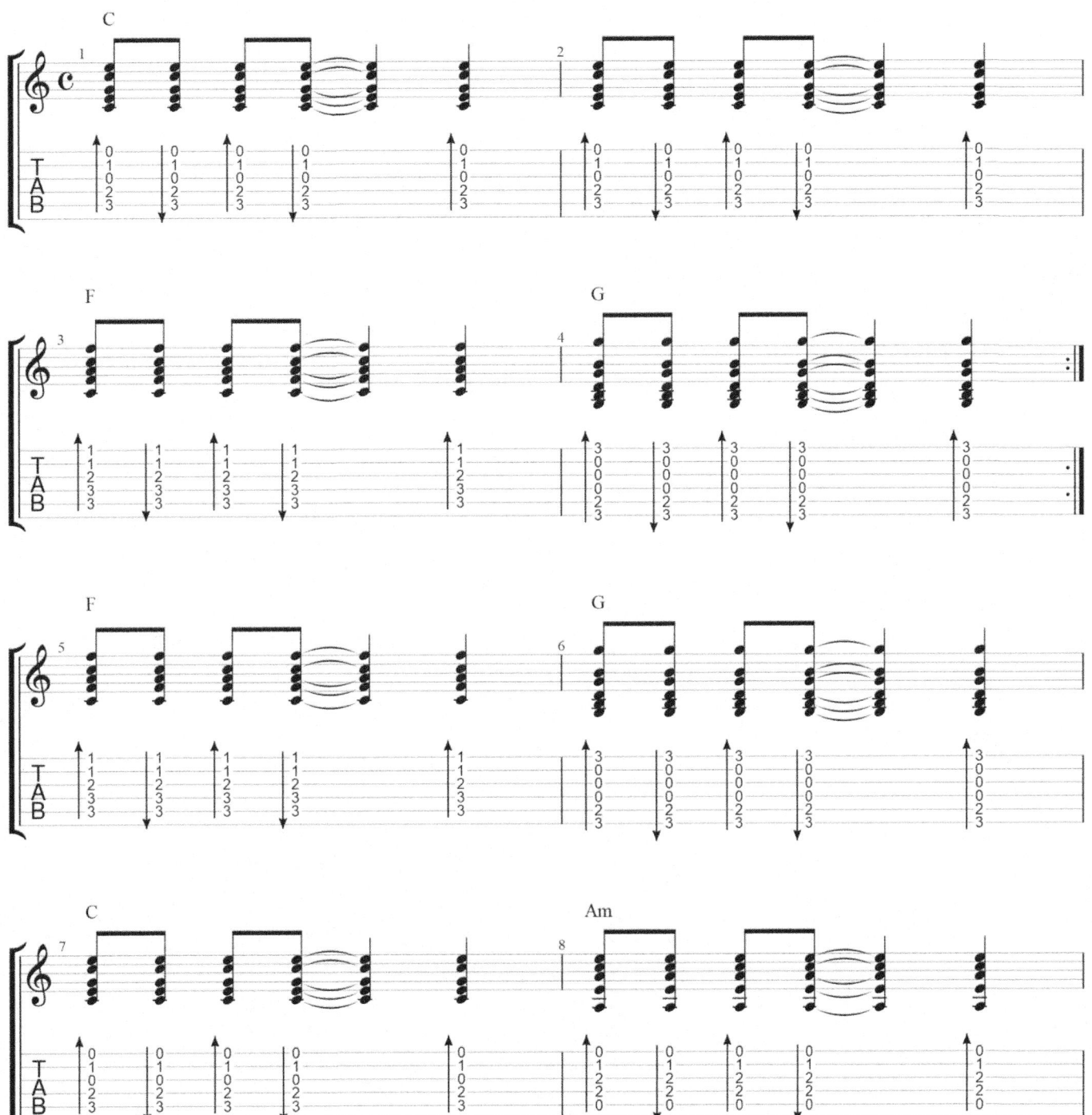

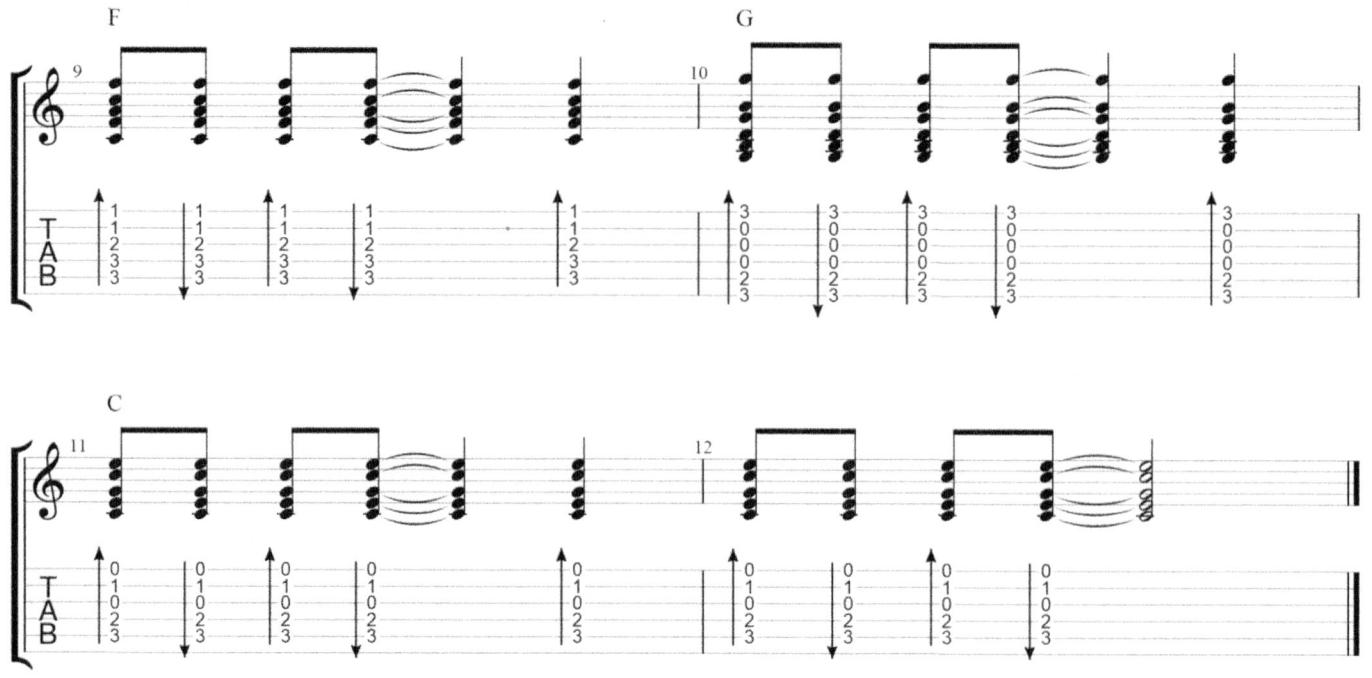

Rhythm 2

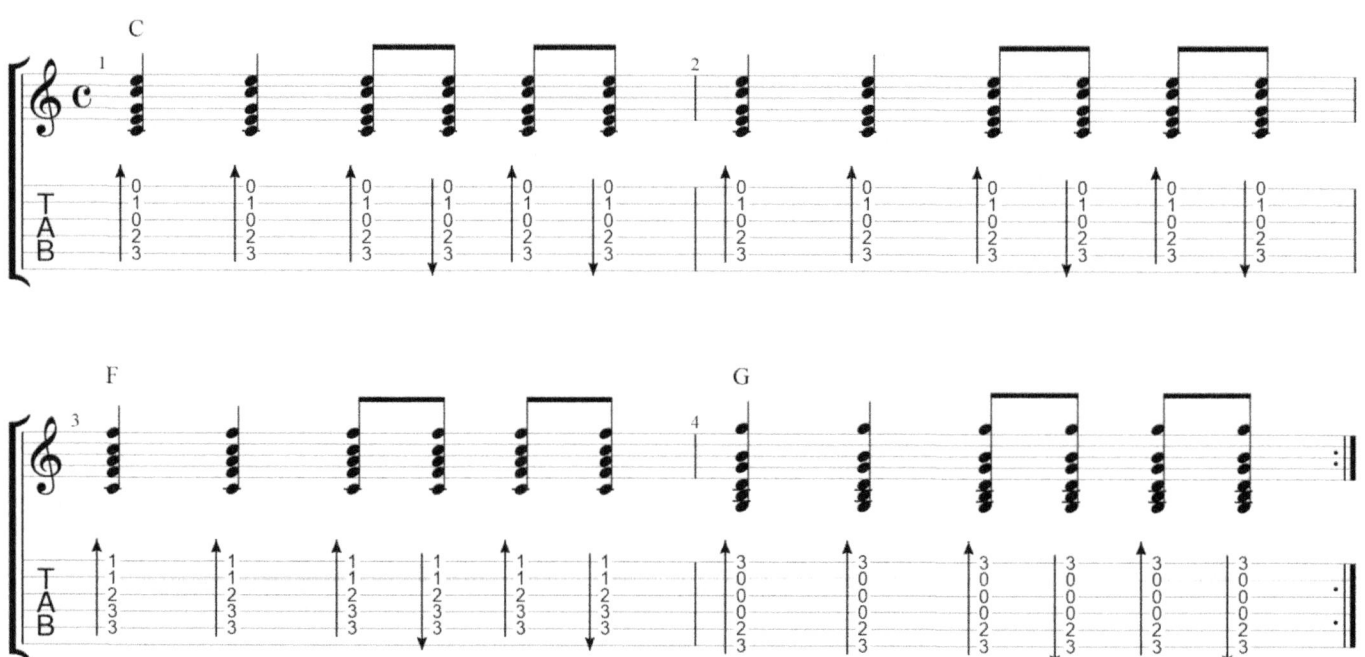

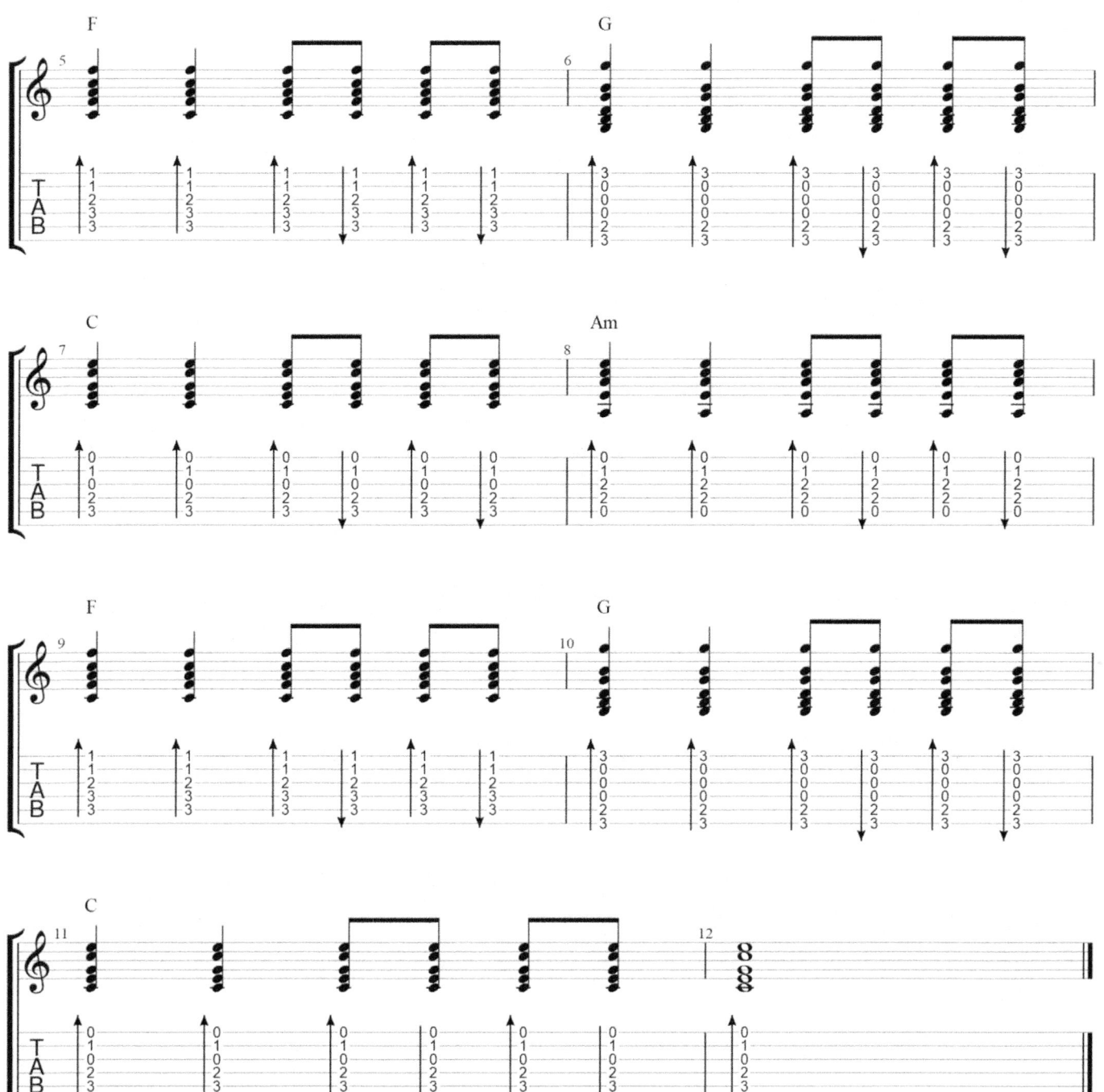

Example Song 5

Medium Country Swing. 4/4 in the key of C with shuffle feel, with muted strums.

Rhythm 1

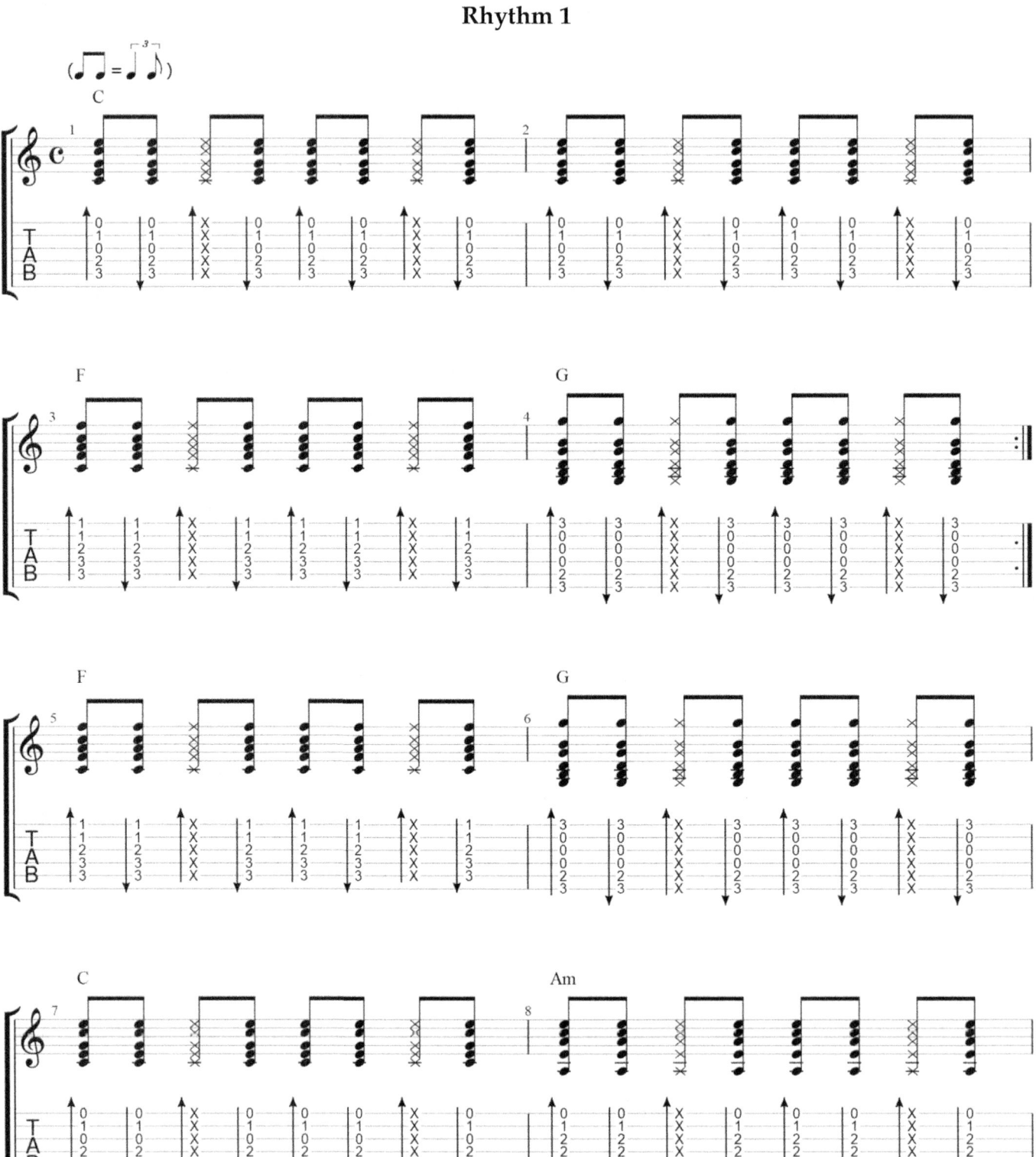

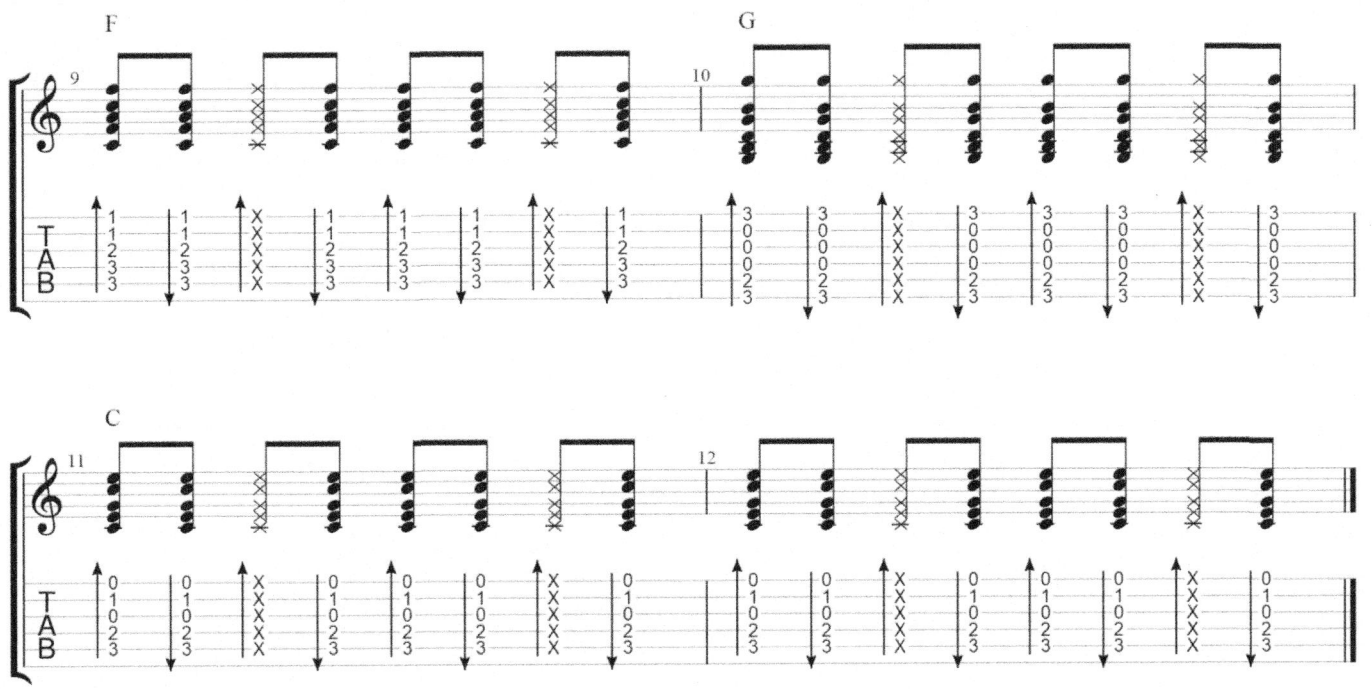

Rhythm 2

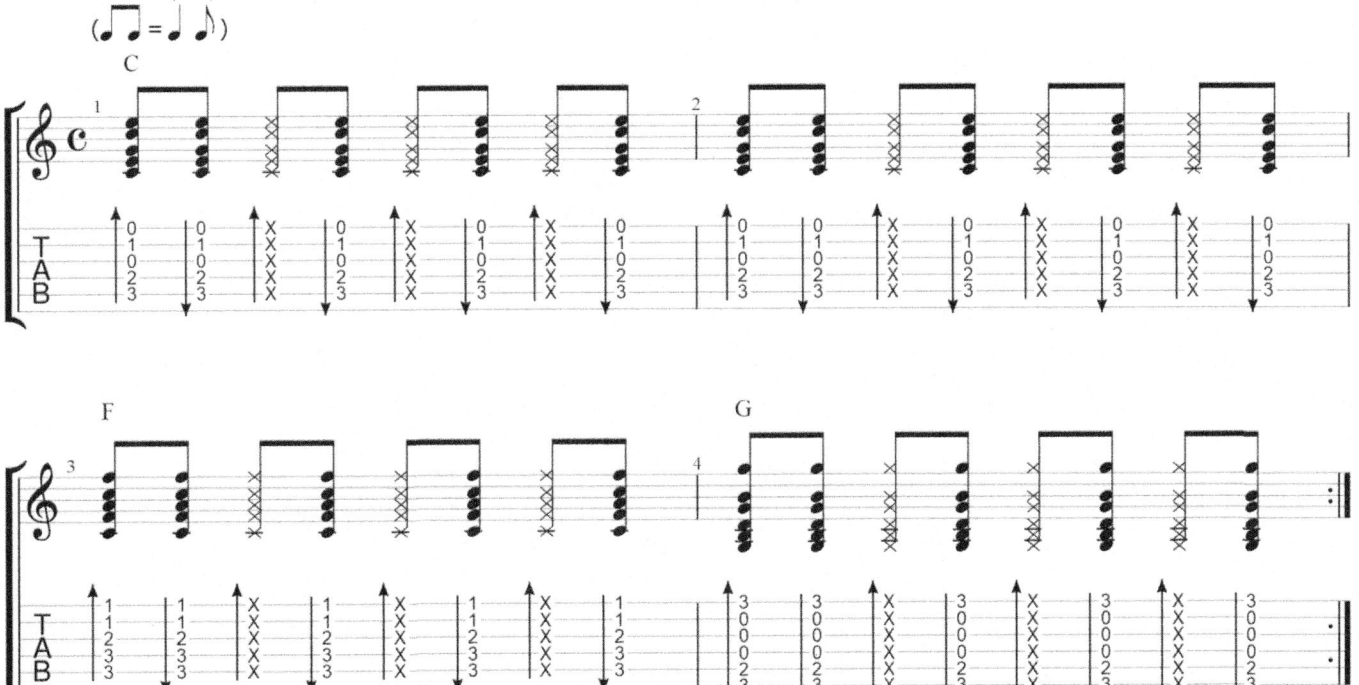

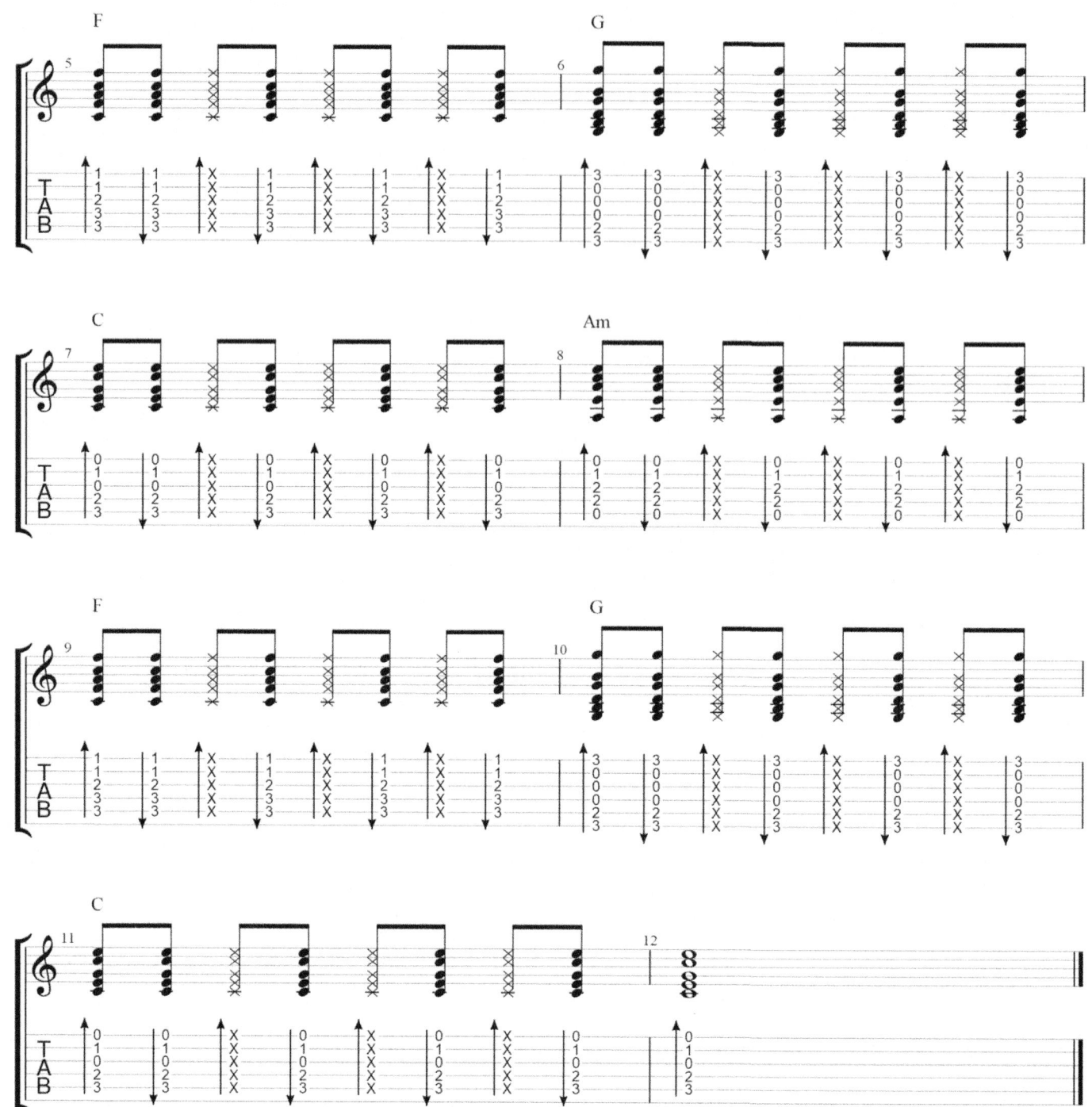

Example Song 6

Medium Tempo Bluegrass. 4/4 in the key of G with straight feel.
This first rhythm is using partial strums. The TAB shows the general idea but it doesn't have to be perfectly accurate, just aim for the bottom or top three strings where show and if you miss a few it doesn't matter.

Rhythm 1

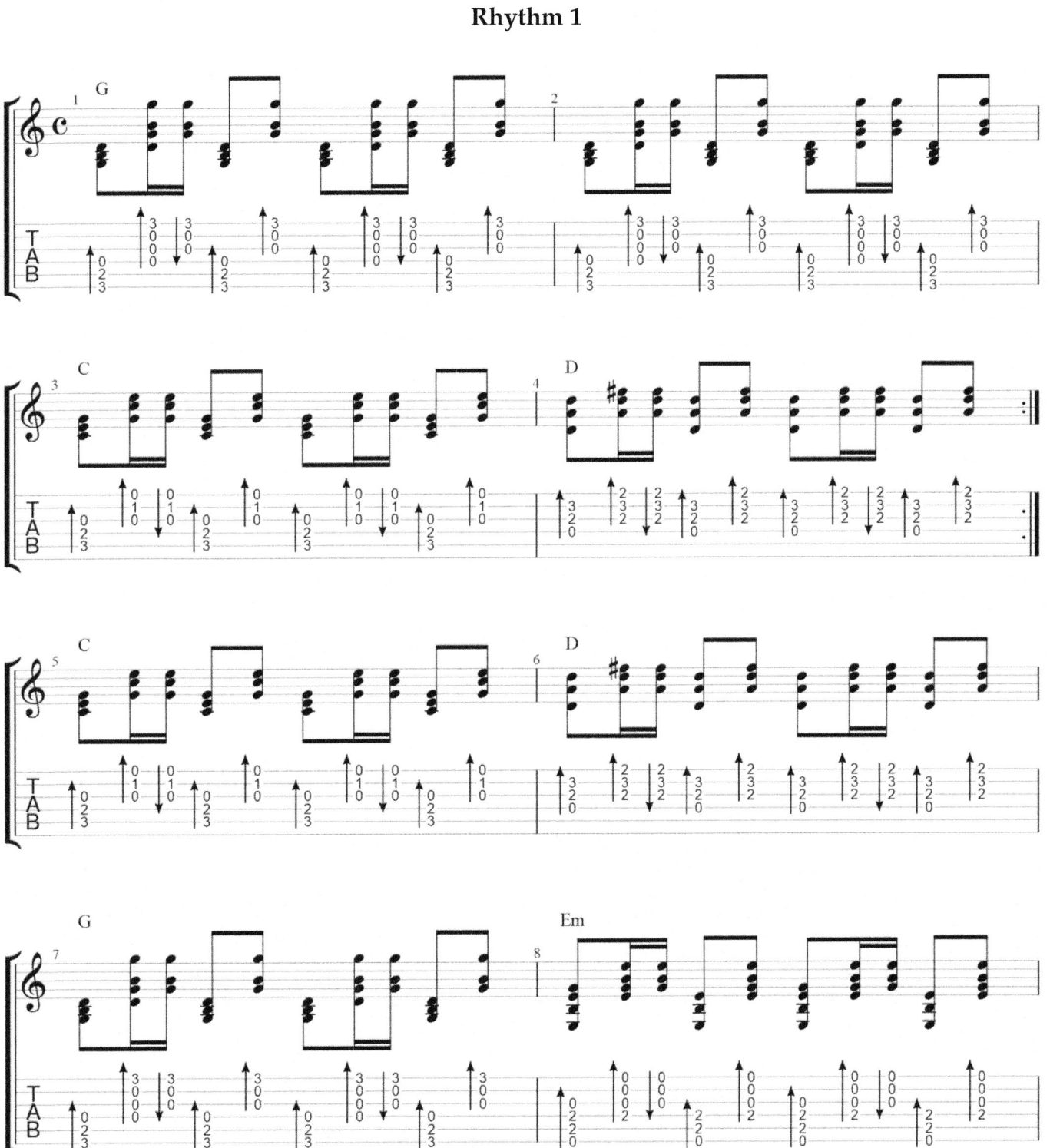

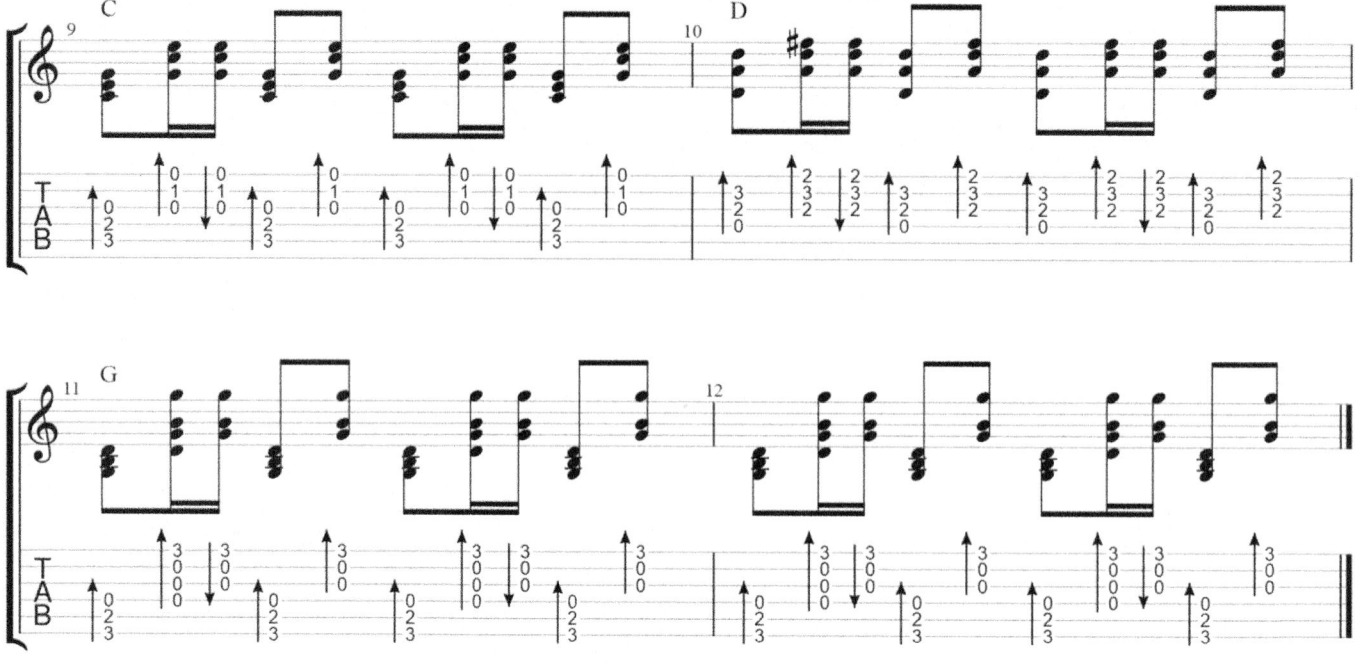

Rhythm 2
Alternating bass. Use all Down Strums

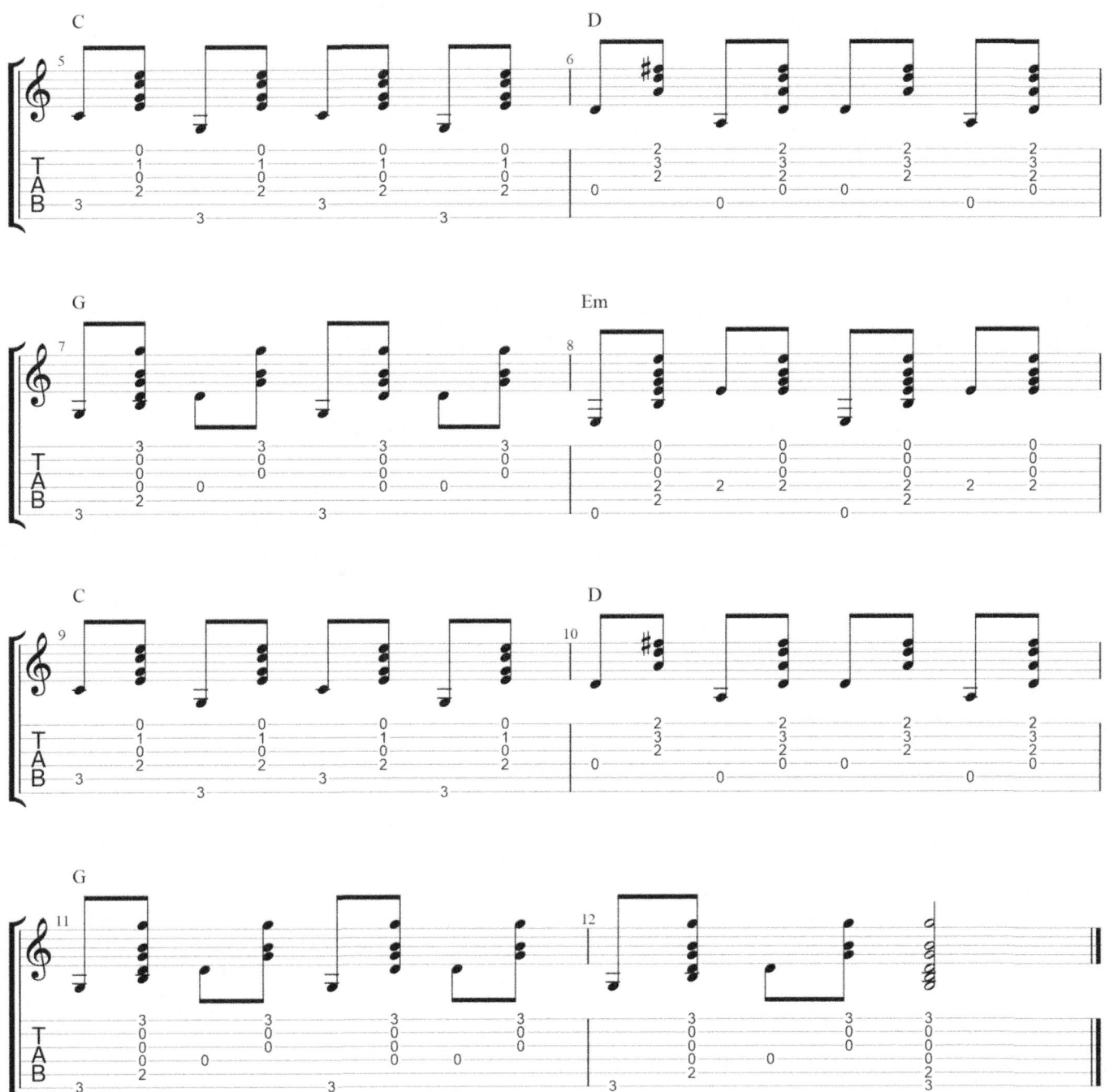

Example Song 7

Slow Country Waltz. 3/4 in the key of G with swing /shuffle feel.

Rhythm 1

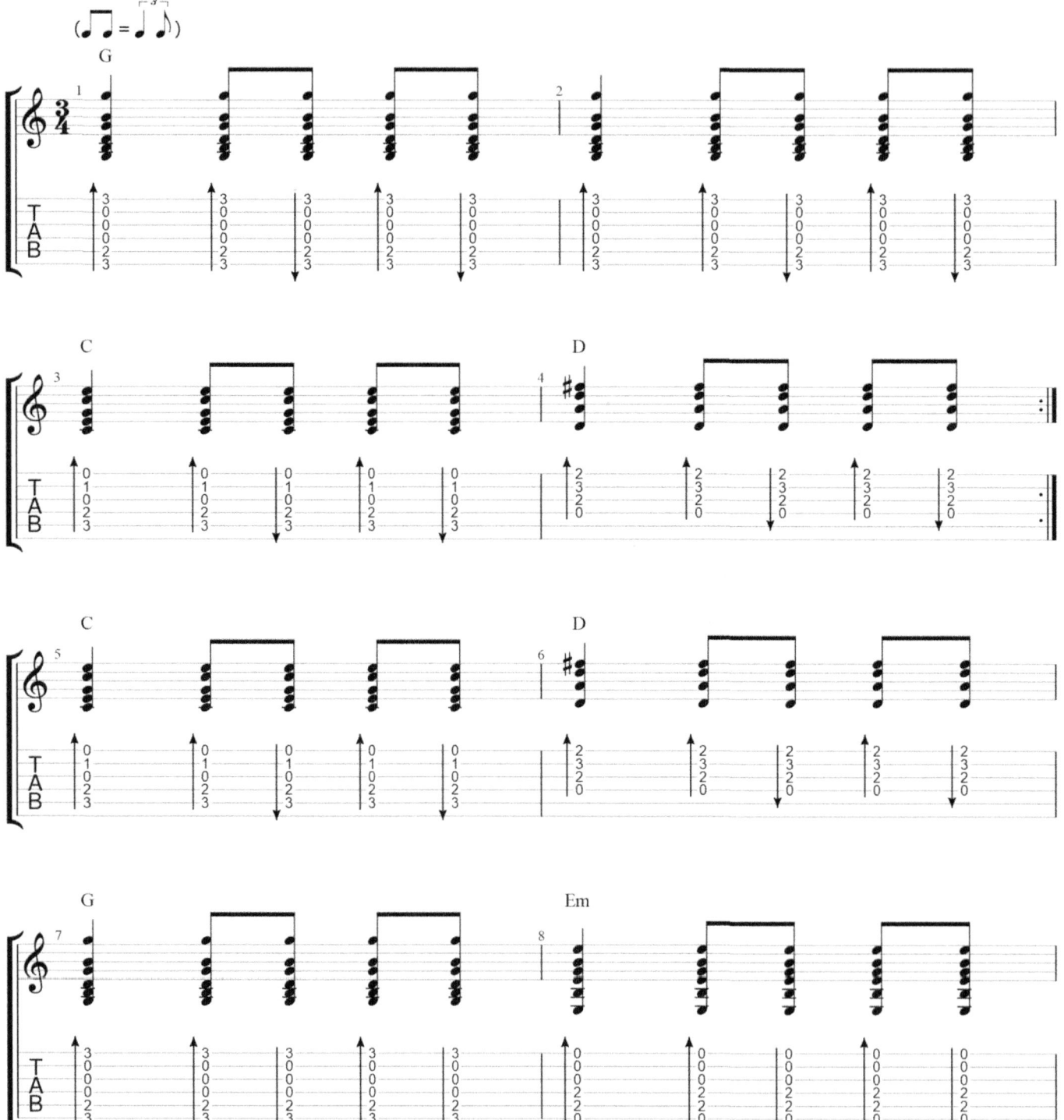

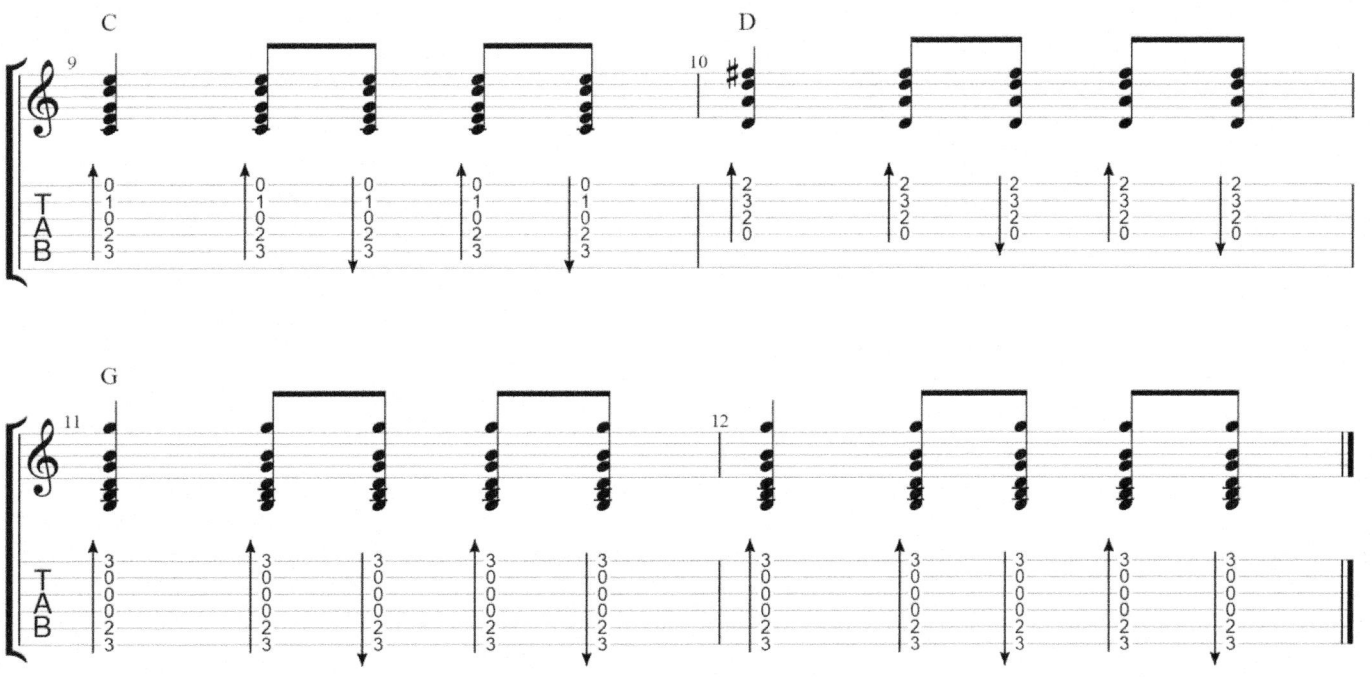

Rhythm 2

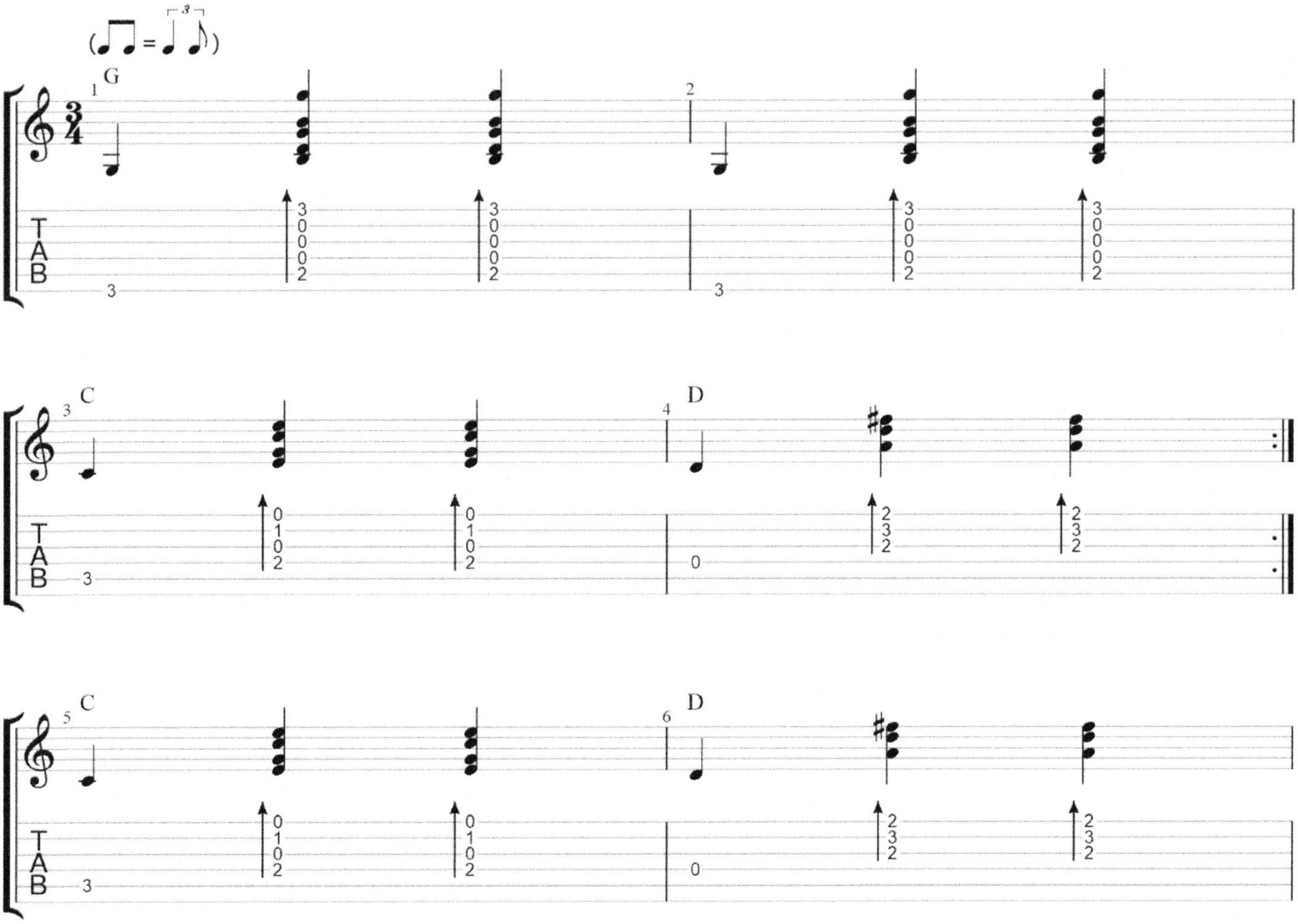

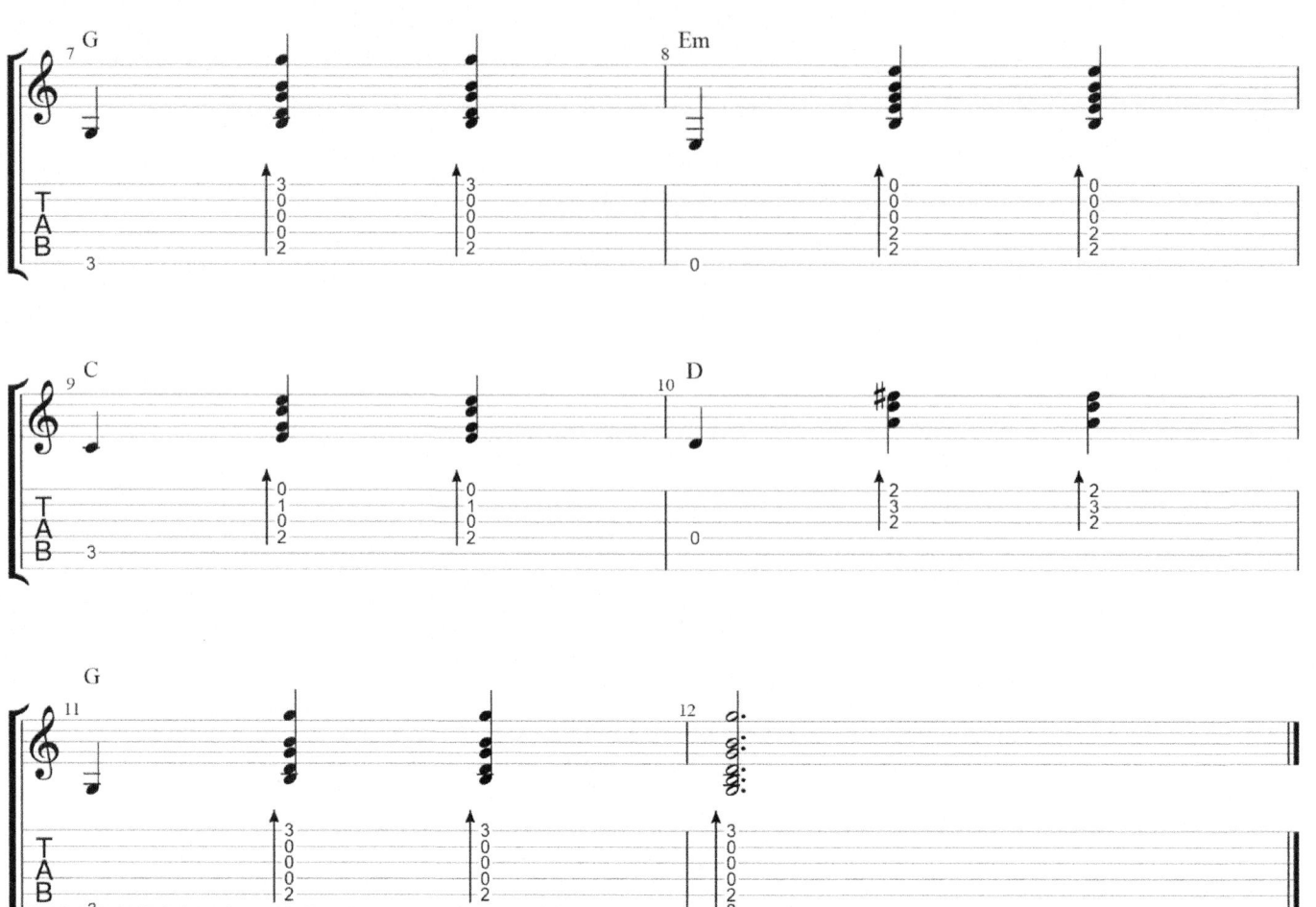

Example Song 8

50s style pop ballad. 6/8 in the key of C with straight feel.

Rhythm 1

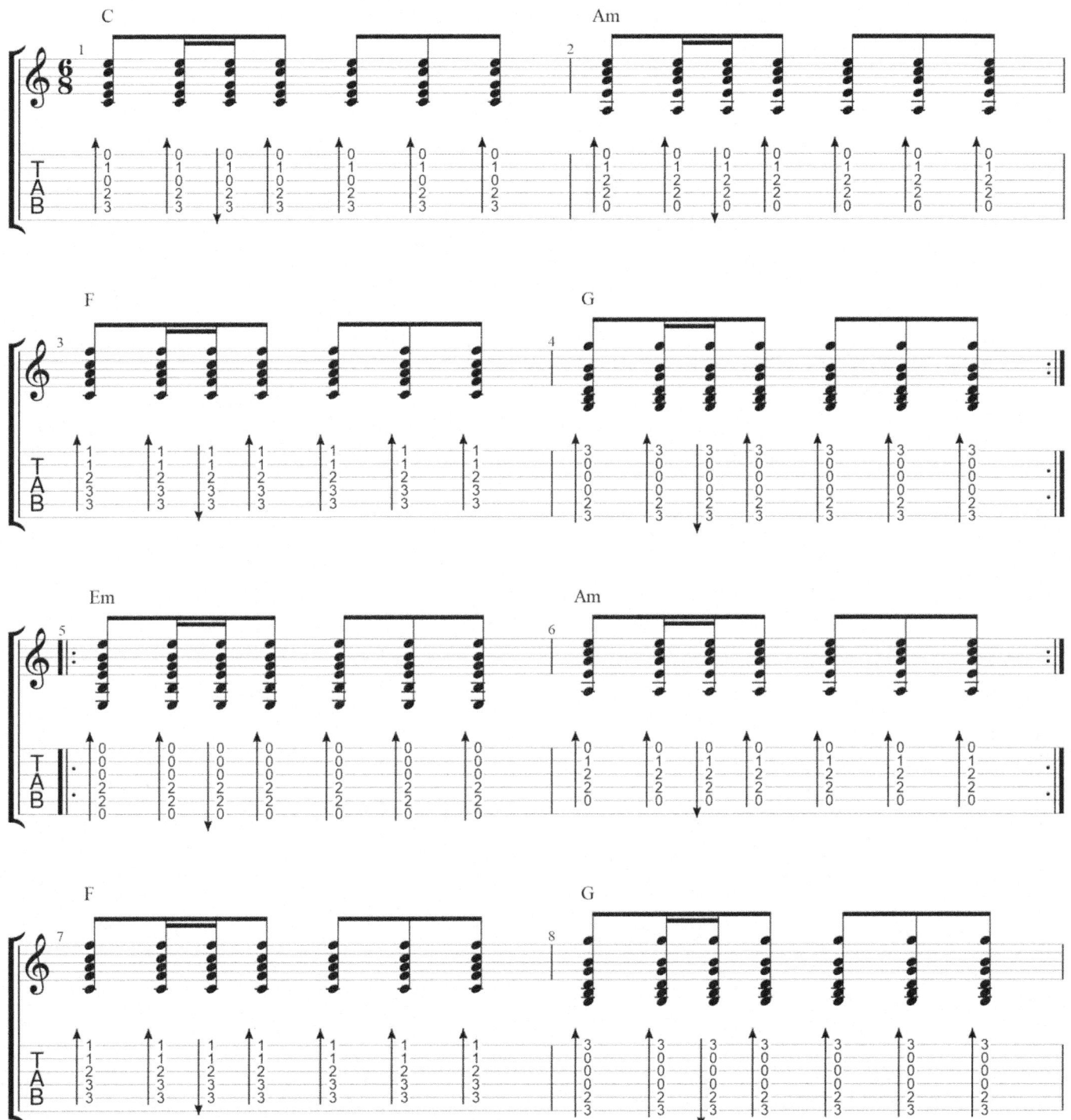

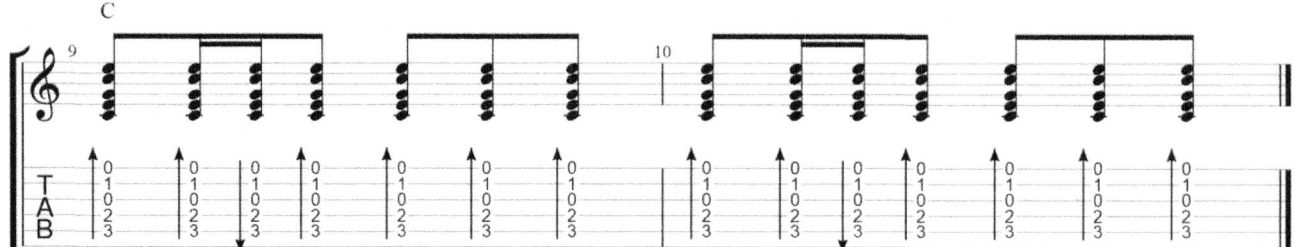

Rhythm 2 – Arpeggios

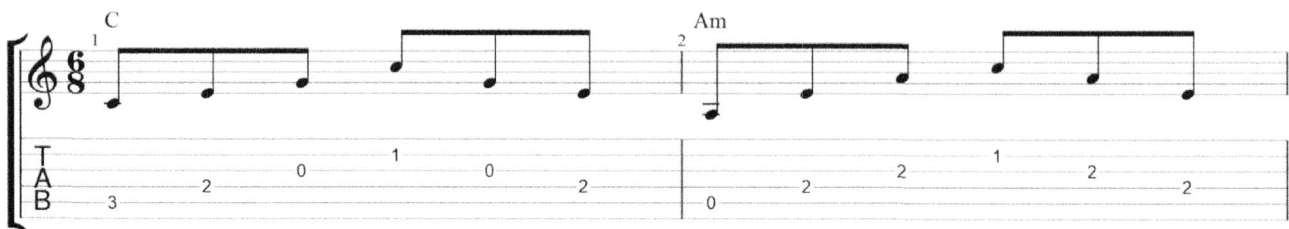
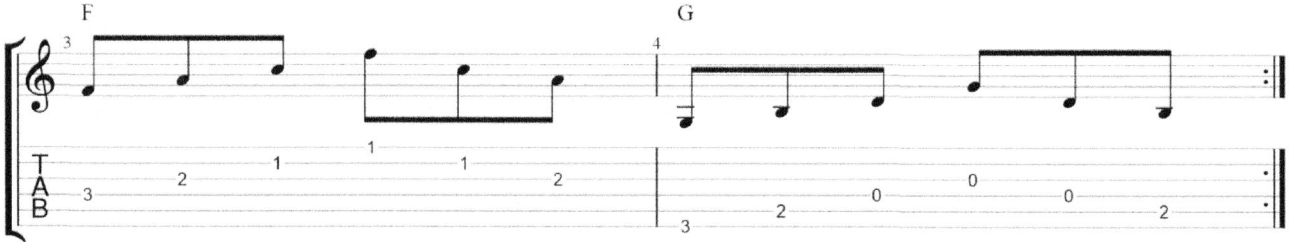
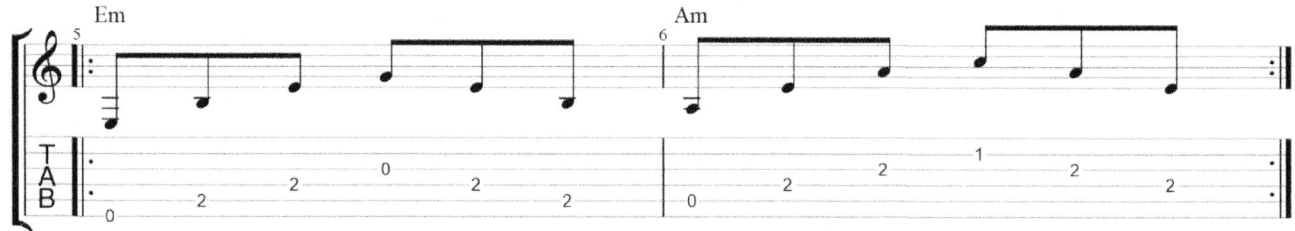
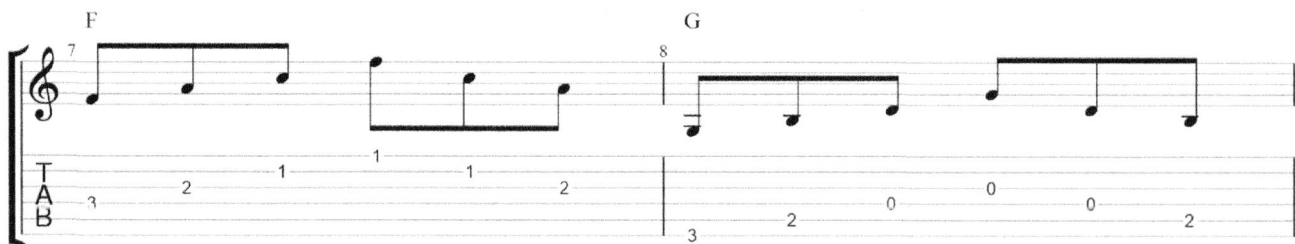
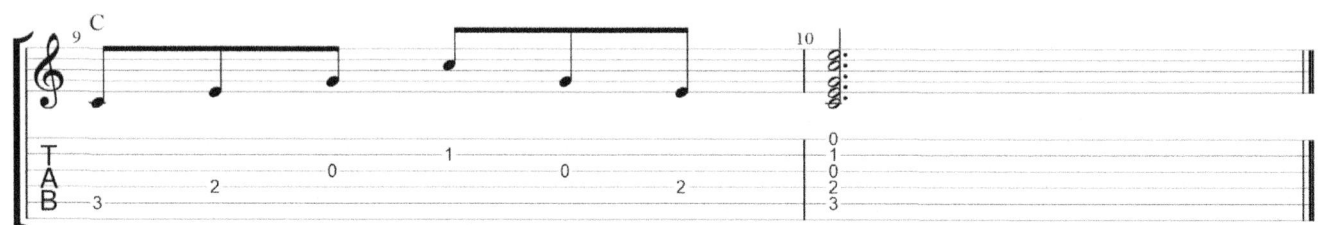

Example Song 9

Slow Blues. 12/8 in the key of A with triplet feel.

Rhythm 1

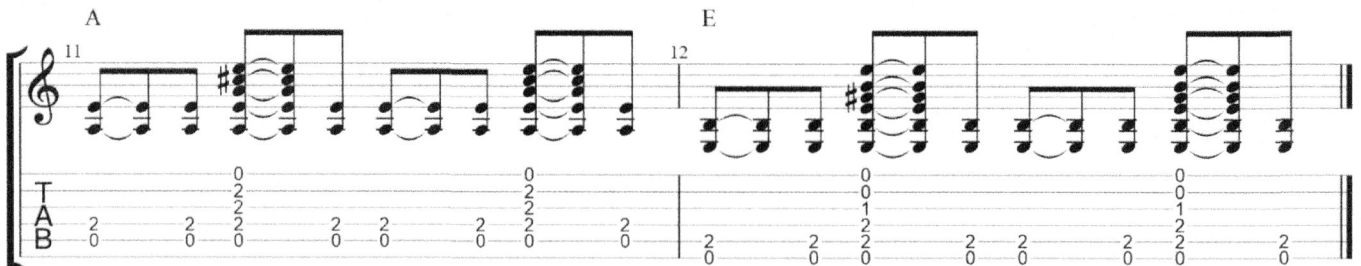

Rhythm 2
All Down Strokes

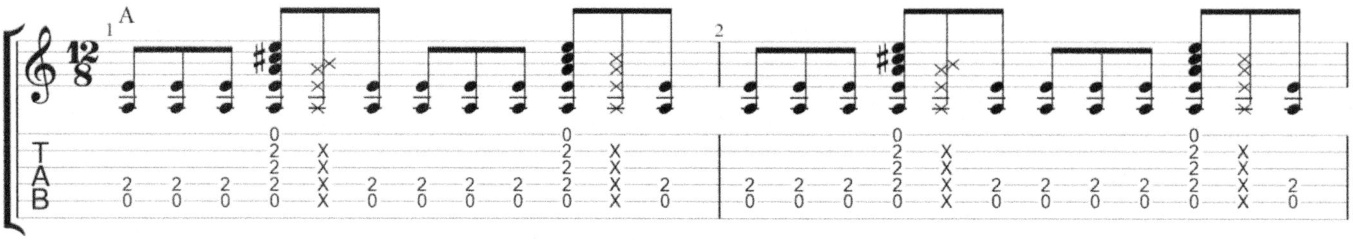

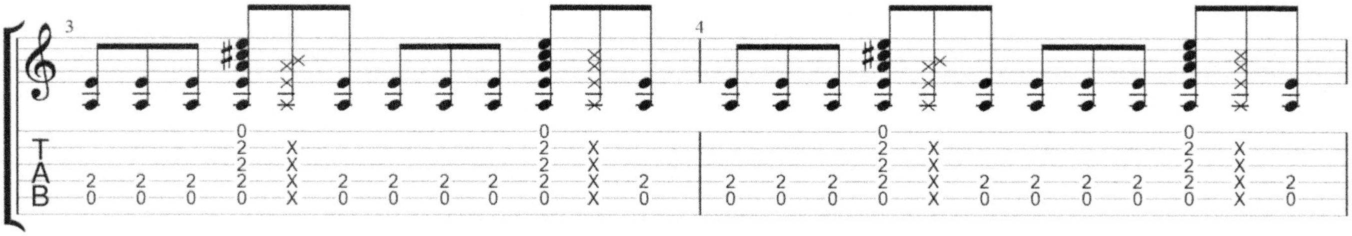

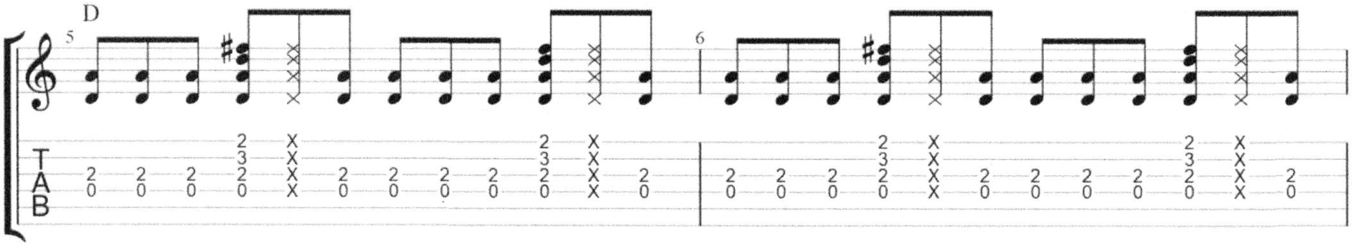

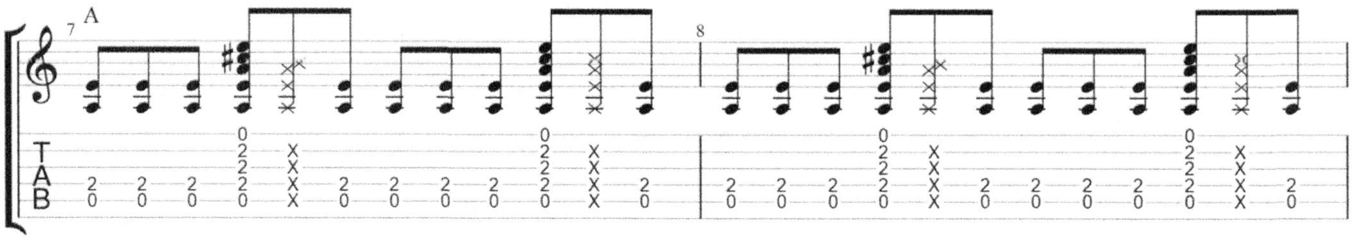

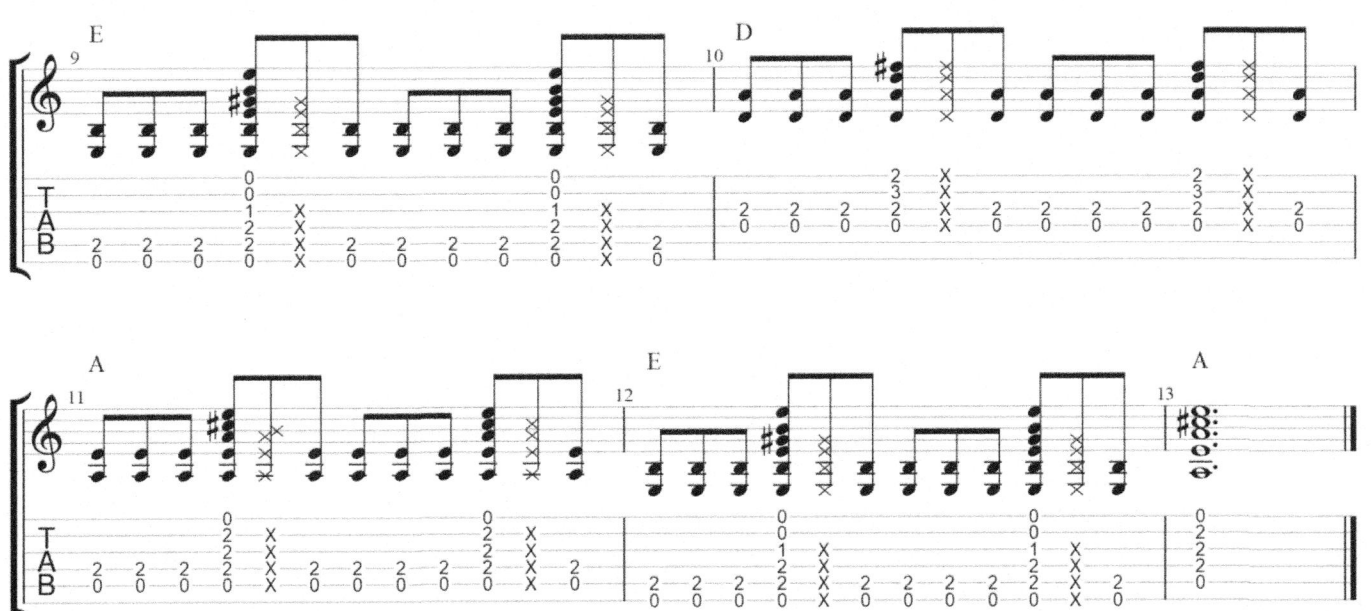

Example Song 10

Slow Blues. 12/8 shuffle in the key of E.

The chords E6 and A6 are used in this rhythm for some melodic variation. They are both quite simple, just finger the A and E chords as normal and then just drop the fourth finger down on the 2nd fret to make the 6 chord. This is made easier by keeping the chord held down the whole time but just play the two strings rhythms where appropriate.

Rhythm 1

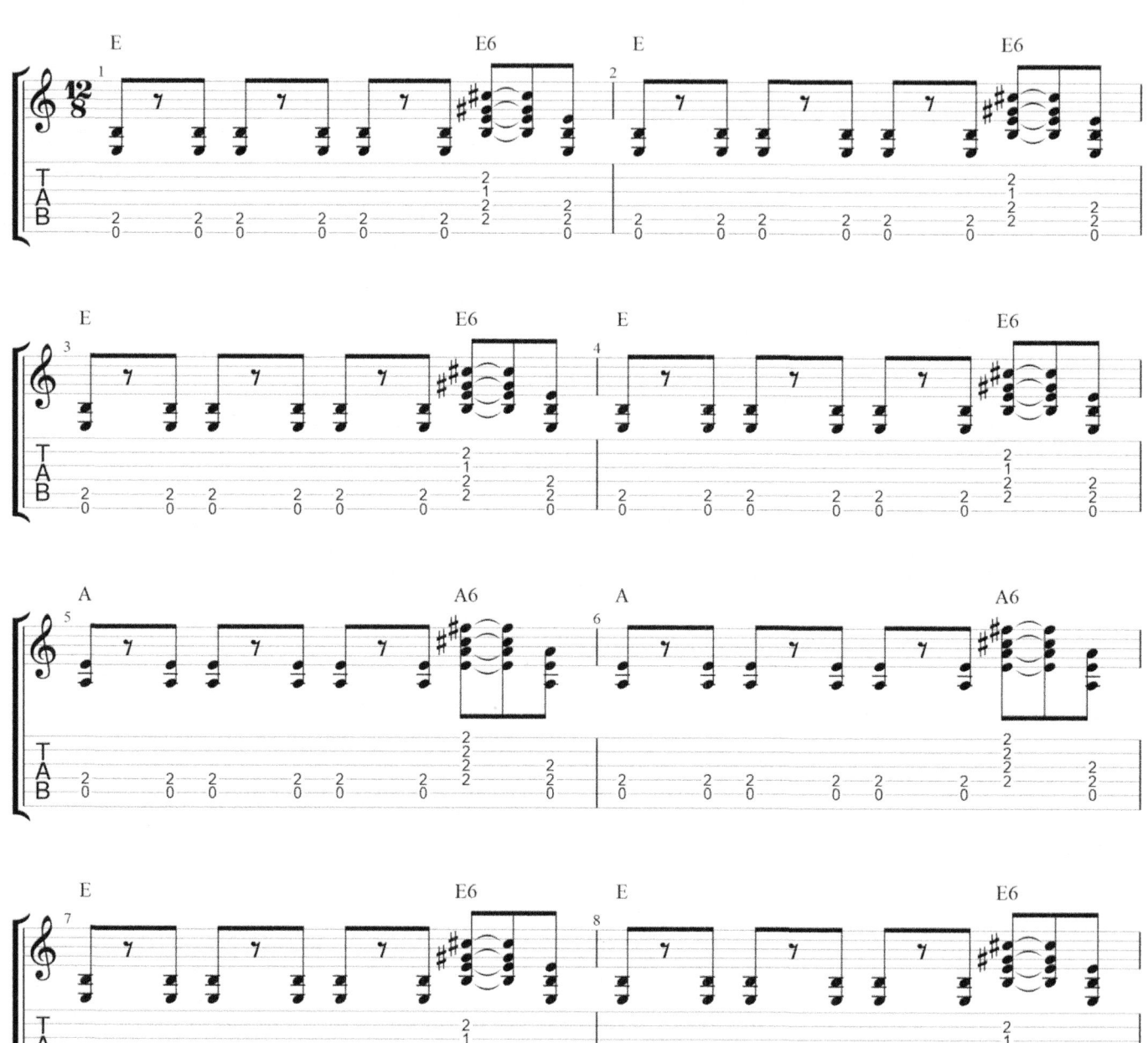

Rhythm 2
Basic Blues Rhythm

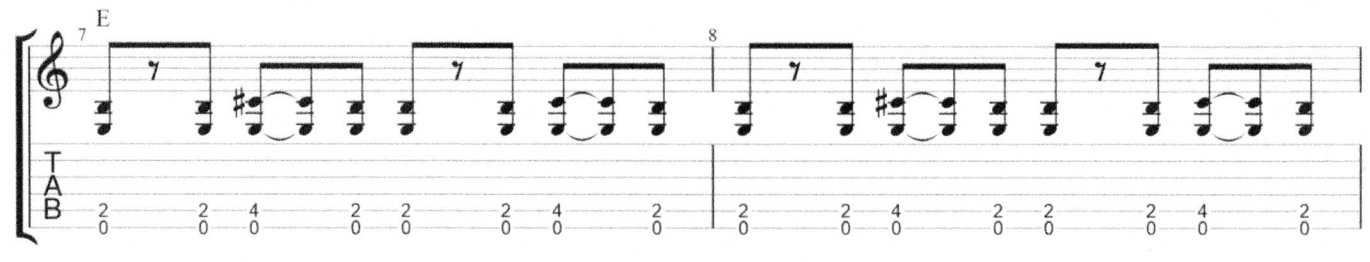
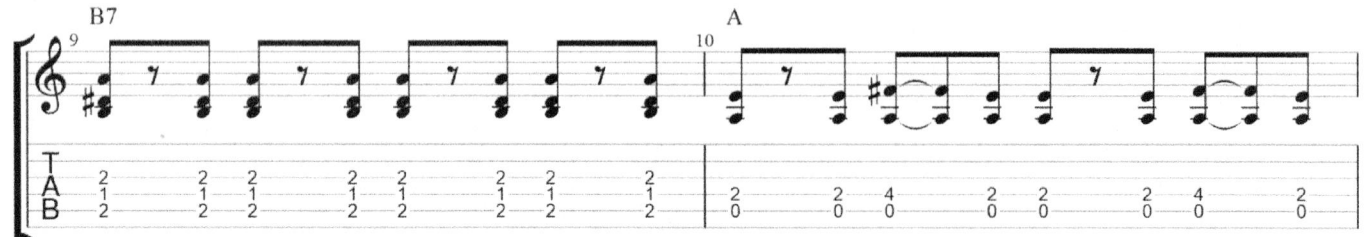
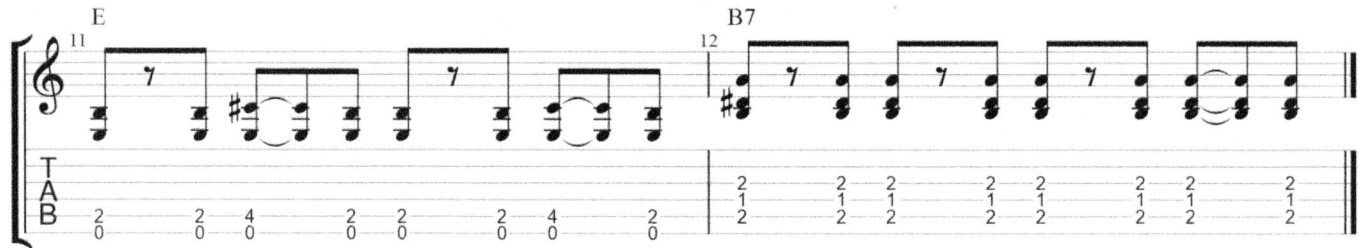

Where Next

Learning and improving is an ongoing process. Continue to practise with the provided backing tracks, keep experimenting with different rhythms and try including some of your own ideas.

Check out my website where you will find more backing tracks and lessons, all on-line for free at the web address shown below. Also check out my Q&A section if you want to ask me anything or just browse other's questions.

Information and Resources

Website:
https://www.guitar-chords.org.uk/

Ask me a question:
https://www.guitar-chords.org.uk/blog/questions/

Newsletter:
https://www.guitar-chords.org.uk/newsletter.html

I also have some free content available which you can find on Soundslice.
https://www.soundslice.com/users/LeeNichols/

Audio Downloads

How to get the audio examples

My philosophy is simple. You've paid for a book with available audio: you should not have to work hard or exchange further information for the audio files. I do not think it's acceptable to force you into giving up your email address in order for you to get what you paid for. I have a newsletter, join it if you want to, but don't expect to hear from me too often, I mostly use it to inform of site updates or the occasional thing I think might be worth sharing.

If you are reading this book on the Kindle App then you may be able to simply click on each example for it to open directly in your browser. Failing that, or if you are reading this in print form, the audio examples for this book are available directly from the web address shown below - no sign-up required. Here you can also download all of the audio examples bundled in zip format and a PDF for the song TABs.

Just go to the website URL below to find the audio examples for this and my other books.

https://www.guitar-chords.org.uk/downloads/

Or directly to the page for this book

https://www.guitar-chords.org.uk/downloads/rhythm-essentials.html

Note: These links will not likely show up in search engines so either click the links above, or type them in full in your browser's address bar.

Printed in Great Britain
by Amazon